"A stimulating and commonsense guide to the coming economic boom. Harry Dent's insight into the nation's economy through the use of demographics is a conceptual breakthrough useful to managers in all types of business. A vital addition to your strategic planning library."
—Richard J. Resch, President, Krueger International

"Harry Dent is a bright, new, emerging economist. He has a fresh and simple approach to forecasting the economy that often goes against the grain. But he is grounded in strong fundamentals of the aging baby boom's spending power. Therefore, I think every forecaster should take a careful look at his unique forecasting methods."
—Robert J. Eggert, Sr., President, Chief Economist, "Blue Chip Economic Indicators"

"Harry Dent's *The Great Boom Ahead* is not just another wake-up call—it is the blueprint for the success of American business. The book compels you to take immediate action . . . or be left in the dust! Must reading for all who want to create the future."
—James A. Finkelstein, President and CEO, W. F. Corroon

"Dent's new book is magnificently heroic! First he says naked demographics will drive economic performance in twenty-first-century North America. Second, between the same covers he offers an astonishing long-range forecast. Figures and dates on the same page! Is Harry on to something, or is he just heroic? Whichever, we cannot afford to ignore this book. Check out Harry Dent."
—Jann W. Carpenter, Professor, Graduate Management Program, Antioch University, Seattle

"Harry Dent's new concepts and forecasting techniques should drive every large and small company's strategic planning efforts in the '90s. Simple to understand, yet deep in its logic, his approach points out the major economic turns to come, the industries to benefit, and the specific marketing and operational strategies to use in order to win."
—James Bandrowski, President, Strategic Action Associates, author, *Corporate Imagination Plus*

"Easy to understand for business managers and entrepreneurs. Practical, down-to-earth. Dent ties a surprising variety of statistics into an exposition that is cohesive and convincing. His concrete examples

and liberal use of illustrations make it easy for the intelligent layman to understand his economic argument. Dent brings complexity into the realm of everyday understanding. This is the kind of viewpoint that should be made available to business people who are faced with making decisions in today's welter of information and uncertainty."
—Mike Van Horn, President Pacific Rim Consortium, author, *Understanding Expert Systems* and *Pacific Rim Trade*

"This is an outstanding book that will benefit anyone wishing to get ahead in the twenty-first century. Harry has a keen perception of economic trends that makes his advice very practical and useful for both large and small businesses."
—O'Neill Wyss, Certified Financial Planner, author, *Strategic Financial Planning for the 1990s*

"I just finished your book, *The Great Boom Ahead*. I found it great reading and very informative. If it prepares the investor for the future as well as your past forecasts warning of the existing recession and the boom in the bond market, then you will have earned your salt. Great job!
—Lloyd M. Mayer, Vice President–Investments, PaineWebber, Kansas City

"Harry Dent is bright, resourceful, thoughtful—a persuasive writer, an economic savant, a practical prophet."
—John Caple, author, *The Ultimate Interview* and *On Purpose*

"In our business of selecting franchise sites demographics is everything. Finally someone has proven how critical it is to forecasting the economy. Mr. Dent has pioneered a brilliant new approach that is wholly appropriate to the new information age."
—Al Pizzurro, founder and CEO, FranSite, San Juan Capistrano, CA

"The best analysis of the economy I have ever read. A brilliant mind with a human values approach. Mr. Dent brings a credible sense of timing to everything from the stock market to inflation to interest rates. We now use his concepts in the timing of all our major investment and management decisions."
—Ronald D. Hunter, CEO, Standard Life Insurance Company of Indiana

THE GREAT BOOM AHEAD

T H E

GREAT

BOOM

AHEAD

*Your comprehensive guide to
personal and business profit in
the new era of prosperity*

Harry S. Dent, Jr.

New York

Library of Congress Cataloging-in-Publication Data

Dent, Harry S.
The great boom ahead : your comprehensive guide to personal prosperity and business profit in the new era of prosperity / by Harry S. Dent, Jr.—1st ed.
p. cm.
ISBN 1-56282-758-8
1. United States—Economic conditions—1981– 2. Economic forecasting—United States. 3. Business cycles—United States. I. Title.
HC106.8.D46 1993
332.024—dc20 92-27601
CIP

Book design by Richard Oriolo

First Paperback Edition

10 9 8 7 6 5 4 3

This book is dedicated to:
My wife, Cee
Nile, Abel, and Iomi
My parents, Harry and Betty Dent

SPECIAL DEDICATION

The greatest epochs in history have often been marked by the emergence of great world teachers. We clearly live in such a period and Da Avabhasa is unquestionably such a teacher. More people should witness the life and teaching of such a spiritual genius. But we prefer to honor such teachers after their lifetime when their fierce criticism of the ego and society can be idealized and avoided. This information age offers the first real opportunity for a great world teacher to be widely heard and recognized while alive. Hold your breath, let go of your religious hopes and ideals, and check out this spiritual teacher. And, of course, expect to be offended as well as inspired.

CONTENTS

PART I

Reinventing Economics—
People Count!

Acknowledgments		ix
1.	The Generation Wave	3
2.	The Spending Wave	21
3.	The Purchasing Power Dividend	47
4.	The Tidal Wave from Tokyo	77
5.	The Innovation Wave	97
6.	The New Customized Economy	129

PART II

How to Profit
in the Growth Boom
of the 1990s

7.	The Global Boom Scenario	157
8.	Investment Strategies for the '90s	180
9.	Growth Markets of the '90s	192
10.	Business Strategies for the '90s	220
11.	Reinventing Corporations	246
	Index	265

ACKNOWLEDGMENTS

I wish to thank my agent, Susan Golomb, for her skills and persistence. Likewise, to Judith Riven, my editor at Hyperion, for her vision and willingness to take a risk on a new book concept. I appreciate Lisa Kitei's valuable contribution to the publicity for this book.

This book's ultimate success will owe much to the writing talents of James V. Smith, Jr. His energetic and down-to-earth style will allow the concepts in this book to reach people at all levels of our society.

I would also like to thank Al Pizzurro for helping to spread the word, Dave Marcadis for his help with technical analysis, and George May for the insights he has given me over the years into the workings of the financial markets.

I extend my best wishes for success to The Executive Committee (TEC) and its members around the world. TEC is an organization that has pioneered what I consider to be the best ongoing education program for executives and CEOs of small- to medium-size businesses. The feedback and interaction I have had in my seminars with their groups has been instrumental in refining my concepts and bringing them into practical application. I especially appreciate the support of Michael Norris and Doug Matthews over the years at TEC.

PART I

REINVENTING ECONOMICS— PEOPLE COUNT!

Getting Ready for the Greatest Boom in History

Part I is for everybody.

Everybody needs to know the new directions we'll be taking in this, the greatest boom since the term was applied to economies. This section introduces and explains all the tools I use to make my predictions. It will tell you of the reasons for the vast increases in purchasing power consumers are about to experience. Although the investment scenarios have been reserved for Part II, you will also read some valuable tips on how to protect yourself against the aftershocks of the coming collapse of Japan's economy.

Finally, you will find in this part of the book the logic that sets up the strategies discussed in Part II.

1

The Generation Wave

New tools predict the greatest boom in history

BULLETIN

Contrary to what most economists say, the economy is highly predictable. New forecasting tools tell of a coming era of prosperity with the Dow reaching as high as 8500 between 2006 and 2010, mortgage rates falling to 5 to 6 percent by 1998, the disappearance of inflation, and the resurgence of America as the premier global economic superpower.

Get ready!

Get ready for an unprecedented economic boom. Forget what some experts are saying about a slow, measured growth of the economy. Forget what the doomsayers are saying about a depression.

I have some welcome news for you, news of a dramatic upswing in the economy, news of a dawning new era of prosperity in which many of you will actually feel wealthy.

Hard to believe? Sure. We've been in a recession. People have been hurt. It's only human to believe that the present climate of uncertainty is going to continue for the foreseeable future and that we'll be mired in a deep recession for the long term.

You just watch. When the economy stumbles again—as I am predicting it will in early- to mid-1993 and likely into 1994—economists, politicians, media pundits, and other so-called experts will once again be spreading reports of gloom and doom.

And why not? All the short-term indicators will be pointing toward a bleak outlook. After all, the economy has been up and down for years. By the time this book is published, we'll probably see stock prices falling. The low interest rates brought on by election-year political moves will likely be reversed in late 1992 or early 1993. The ensuing downturn will reinforce deep pessimism that there's something fundamentally wrong with our country's economy.

As this recession tends to worsen in 1993, some experts will begin whining about the onslaught of the next Great Depression.

They will be wrong! There will most emphatically not be a Great Depression of the '90s. Although this will seem to be the case when the recession worsens dramatically after the election.

This final phase of the 1990 to 1993/1994 recession is just the last nasty dose of medicine to prepare us for the most potent phase of the greatest economic boom in our history. I'm not talking about a short-term spike. And I'm not forecasting slow, measured growth. The economy will soon come screaming out of this recession for good, growing in leaps—with only brief corrections—into the next century.

Yes, the recession of the early 1990s will reverse itself even more abruptly than it did after the 1980 to 1982 recession, when an incredible boom followed, accompanied by a drop in interest rates. Remember? From 1982 to 1990 we had a burgeoning economy that surprised almost everybody—in fact, by 1992 stocks had more than quadrupled in value. That boom would have been entirely predictable using my forecasting tools, if they'd been developed at the time.

The coming boom will be even more astonishing in its intensity, its length, and in the heights it reaches. So while we are gutting out this severe, temporary slump we should be preparing for the great surprise of our times—a long, unprecedented boom—without inflation!

So . . . what about the recession itself?

Simple. The recession was meant to be. It was a natural step in the life of the economy, a predictable, necessary component of change as we move from a decaying economy into a new one full of vitality.

Since 1988, using my own simple but powerful forecasting tools, I have been predicting a prolonged recession with deflation in real estate and chaos in the banking system. I have pushed my consulting and speaking clients to use this recession as an opportunity to reorganize their companies for a productivity leap. I have encouraged executives to reinvent corporate innovation. I have warned them to shift strategic focus in time for a new economy.

In short, I have continually stressed the more critical long-term boom trends, arguing that our downturn would last two to three years. I have described this recession as the final blow to inflation, ushering in a revitalized period of low interest rates and lower prices as baby boomers enter their peak spending years.

It gives me no pleasure to see so much economic ruin in the

downside predictions as they come true. To those people who have been hurt, I say, "Take heart. The recession's end is coming by late 1994. Get ready for a new era of prosperity and affluence."

Boom times?

Absolutely. I tell people, "I know you don't like the sound of this, but if we just let this 'deflation crisis' happen, the positive effect of lower prices and dropping interest rates will make it all worthwhile." Tom Peters may have called the theme of the 1980s correctly in *Thriving on Chaos,* but the 1990s and beyond will be different. Economic trends are far more predictable than people think. Interest rates will drop. Inflation—that great tax we have all been paying for decades—will vanish. We will see dramatic improvements in our living standards, in our purchasing power, and in the quality of our lives. I tell people the Dow Jones will at least quadruple from its bottoming process between late 1993 and 1994.

I tell them to get ready.

The response is always the same, always the narrowed gazes and lifted eyebrows. People look at me as if I might be crazy, because my scenario differs so much from that of the conventional wisdom of economic forecasters. But rarely do they discount my predictions entirely. They feel that instinctive human optimism of the no-man's-land that falls between hope and despair, that moment's hesitation that holds off raising the question: *"How do you know?"*

They want proof. They want concrete evidence that better times are ahead. They want to find a reason to look to the future with hope rather than despair. To share my evidence and my optimism with them and you is the reason I wrote this book.

So here's a simple, pivotal discovery from my years of research as a businessman and consultant to companies on the leading edge of technologies and systems of management. This discovery that will change the way we do business is . . .

The economy is highly predictable!

That's right, I have used a set of entirely new economic measuring instruments that establish—contrary to what most people believe—that the economy is predictable. Using new forecasting tools as dependable as actuarial tables are in the insurance industry, I predict a "Roaring '90s" lasting into the next century. I have even formulated a specific timetable. I'm confident enough to call the benchmark highs and lows in interest rates, inflation, and the stock market.

You need these tools to profit in the coming boom by making well-informed decisions about your business, your work, and your personal investments.

The downturn thus far has been harsh, but the boom beginning sometime in 1994 won't necessarily be easy. Even as it ushers in many welcome changes, this boom will also introduce a unique set of complications—an accelerated rate of change and a vigorous state of competition. In one sense, you are going to need . . .

An economic survival kit

This book provides the information and personal management tools you will need to adapt to boom times. Here are some of the practical applications for your business and personal life:

- A clearly defined United States and global economic forecast
- Investment portfolio recommendations
- Types of stocks in any industry to invest in
- Growth markets of the 1990s for businesses
- Major social and cultural trends
- Business strategies for attacking growth markets

- Methods of organizing companies for new ways of doing business
- A preview of how our jobs and organizations will change

But how can anybody predict the economy?

If I were to answer that it's magic, you would dismiss me altogether. If I were to say it was my trade secret developed in research as a follow-on to my Harvard MBA, you would still dismiss me altogether . . . just a little less politely.

So I'll tell you that it's not magic. And it's not a trade secret. It's a simple process of examining factors that are completely within the ken of average understanding. You don't need complex computer models and a Harvard MBA. Understanding the economy is a matter of recognizing its fundamental simplicity.

The economy is not beyond comprehension

Here's a simple diagram that summarizes the principles I will be addressing. I call this diagram the Generation Wave. The four related waves represent factors that determine the direction of the economy.

The Generation Wave shows how a generation affects the economy in all its aspects as it ages. Every generation progresses through a predictable cycle. As it grows up, it spawns innovations in new technologies and social values. Then, as it moves into adulthood, it uses its earning and spending power to adopt these innovations, creating a boom cycle in the economy. Finally, as the generation enters its maturing years, it controls investments and

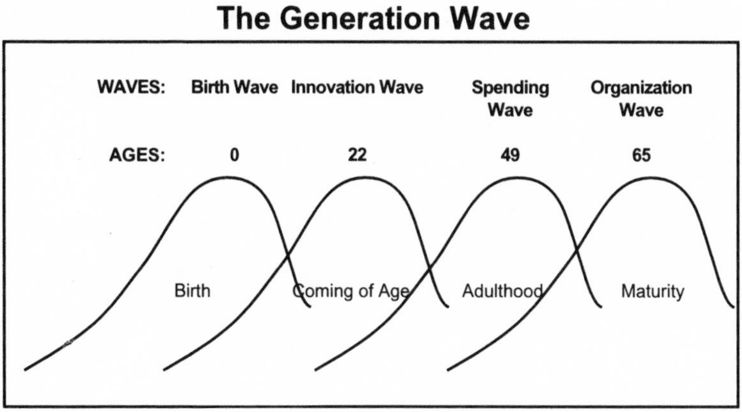

The Generation Wave

WAVES: Birth Wave   Innovation Wave   Spending   Organization
                                            Wave   Wave

AGES: 0   22   49   65

Birth   Coming of Age   Adulthood   Maturity

Figure 1-1. The Generation Wave

corporate and political power, which it uses to change organizations and institutions.

That's the Generation Wave in general. Now let's look at the baby boom's Generation Wave in particular.

In Figure 1-2 you can see that the baby boom generation was born as a wave peaking between 1957 and 1961. The next wave shows the generation coming of age in the late 1970s and early 1980s, innovating and embracing new social values and critical new technologies such as microcomputers, which were then in their entrepreneurial stage. The third wave represents the boom period—the peak period of spending—as the baby boom generation progresses predictably up a steep earning and spending curve until it reaches a peak at around age 49. This is when baby boomers adopt new technologies and products into the mainstream. When this happens, the new technologies experience a growth explosion, supplanting old technologies with the same vigor with which automobiles replaced railroads as the primary industry in the Roaring Twenties.

Finally, the baby boom generation moves into the power structure of business and industry from their 40s to their 60s, bringing about dramatic changes in how we structure the nature of work

The Baby Boom Generation Wave

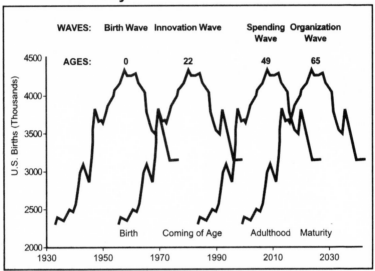

Figure 1-2. The Baby Boom Generation Wave

and our organizations. From 1994 to 2010 the Spending Wave and new technology adoption rate will accelerate toward a peak while our organizations enter an era of innovation and change much as our new products and technologies did in the '70s and '80s.

You can trace this generation cycle all the way back in our nation's history with the help of a book called *Generations,* by William Strauss and Neil Howe. For example, the last generation, which I call the Bob Hope generation, was born between 1897 and 1924. In their innovation cycle in the 1930s and 1940s they gave us the A-bomb, television, the mainframe computer, the jet engine, radar, new home appliances like the automatic washer and dryer, power equipment on automobiles, and consumer electronics. This generation fought World War II. With their Spending Wave we got the boom of the '50s and '60s. And since the '60s this generation has dominated our political and corporate institutions from Eisenhower to Bush in the presidency—with the command and control management style they learned in World War II.

The Generation Wave represents the book's premise, namely:

We are moving into the greatest economic boom in history, not because of anything government or industry or individuals are planning to do, but because of fundamental trends already set in motion by the baby boom generation. These effects will be felt most powerfully in the next decade when the Spending Wave, the Innovation Wave, and the Organization Wave come together in a powerful confluence. Such patterns and cycles of spending, innovation, and organization are fully predictable. Using them as tools, you can accurately forecast the direction of the economy.

Here's a brief summary of how each of these waves works.

The Spending Wave

The earning and spending cycle of a generation affects economic booms and busts most dramatically. This is the subject of Chapter 2. My research shows a simple fact that has been largely ignored. We know precisely when we as consumers will spend—on average by age. A generation of people spends and saves and works and matures in predictable patterns as it ages. If you know when people will spend, you can predict the economy—it's that simple!

Patterns of spending behavior for specific generations—especially large ones—have observable outcomes for the economy. These outcomes can be charted and projected into the future. This gives us a tool with the power to predict economic trends. You see, the average family's spending reaches its peak presently around age 49. The larger the generation, the greater the effect of that spending peak. You can take any generation, examine its

birth rate, and project that birth rate 47 years (Bob Hope generation) to 49 years (baby boom generation) ahead. Then you can
pinpoint the time when the birth rate will have its effect on our
economy. As I indicated earlier, the effects of the Spending Wave
of the Bob Hope generation, born between 1897 and 1924, were
felt in the boom of the 1950s and 1960s. In fact, the Bob Hope
generation's birth rate, projected 47 years ahead, parallels the
performance of the Standard & Poor 500 Index so closely that it
cannot possibly be coincidence.

Think about the effect of the baby boom generation. This largest
generation of births in our history is far from its peak in earning
and spending. As it approaches this peak, it will have a dramatic impact on the economy, creating the greatest boom in our
history.

The Innovation Wave

A second powerful tool shown in the Generation Wave is the Innovation Wave, which is closely related to the Spending Wave.

The Innovation Wave outlines how new technologies are innovated and adopted. Innovations age and follow their own life cycles
just as people do. An innovation experiences its birth and adolescence in an entrepreneurial phase. Next, new technologies go
through a dramatic growth phase as the innovations are adopted
into the mainstream by the generation that innovated the technologies—as they accumulate the purchasing power. Finally, the
innovations mature and flatten out as new technologies are born
to supplant them. The remarkable thing about this Innovation Wave
is that the timetable and degree of these phases is fundamentally
predictable. That means you can use the timetable as another
forecasting tool.

In Chapter 5, I show how the Innovation Wave predicts the
life span of technologies. A new technology will spend the same
amount of time in its entrepreneurial phase, expanding from 0 to

10 percent of its market, as it will in its growth phase, expanding from 10 percent to 90 percent. This tool helps identify products and innovations that will replace more established, mature products. A simple tool called the S-Curve allows you to chart the life span of new products and technologies as they move into the economy.

That's a powerful insight. For example, what if you had known in advance the timetable for radials to capture the tire market? What if you had been able to predict when compact discs would replace record albums? If you were in the tire or record business, what would that have meant to you? If you were an astute investor, what would it have meant to know exactly where to put your money?

Here's another remarkable finding of my research . . .

Periods of inflation and deflation are predictable! That's right, there's finally a rational explanation for inflation's existence, duration, and intensity.

What if you knew inflation's timetable? You could have foreseen the inflationary 1970s and 1980s. You would have known when to seek investments in real estate and gold to hedge against inflation.

I'll show you how inflationary periods typically occur during times of high investment and low productivity as old technologies begin to falter. You'll see why it takes a large investment to incorporate a new generation into the work force. As the Spending Wave brings new technology into the mainstream, inflation increasingly disappears. The disappearance of inflation will create an incredible purchasing power dividend in the coming two decades.

Understanding deflation is every bit as important. As deflationary times approach, you'll understand why companies are folding, because they aren't efficient enough to compete in times of falling prices. With such knowledge, you could have foreseen slumping real estate prices in the late '80s and early '90s.

In the longer-term future, you'll be able to start protecting yourself against severe deflationary periods—those times we call depressions. All this information about inflation and deflation is in Chapter 3.

Chapter 4 addresses the global effects of the economic collapse of Japan, what I call "The Tidal Wave from Tokyo." Japan will fail almost as dramatically as the USSR because centralized planning cannot succeed in the information age.

In Chapter 6, I show how the Innovation Wave generates predictable growth cycles in business and industries. Once we understand how the Innovation and Spending Waves interact, we can predict global and investment scenarios, subjects of Chapters 7 and 8.

Chapters 9 and 10 address how business can take advantage of the growth industries that will be generated by the innovation and spending of the baby boom generation.

The Organization Wave is addressed in Chapter 11. Understanding how one generation makes an innovative impression on its own culture is useful. Such knowledge becomes a tool that allows you to make sound assumptions about how business will have to be conducted in dealing with the new generation. Of course, these kinds of organizational effects have already begun to be felt in many kinds of businesses, as Tom Peters has emphasized in his blockbuster books. Steve Jobs at Apple, Bill Gates at Microsoft, and T. J. Rodgers at Cypress Semiconductor are three examples of heroes of our times.

You will soon be reading about many more such entrepreneurial men and women who lead and manage better than the hierarchical managers of the previous generation. The real power shift is going to start in the mid-1990s at about the same time the effects of the Spending Wave, the Innovation Wave, and the Organization Wave are going to be converging in strength. So all these effects will be combined.

That's why the coming economic boom is going to be so powerful, so competitive, and so full of changes.

The Bottom Line

As I take you through all my reasoning and research, I'll show you how I arrived at my conclusions about the economy. I will share dozens and dozens of statistics and examples that prove my claims. But first, here's . . .

A preview of Harry Dent's Projected Economic Scenario
- The Dow plummets to lows in the range of 1700 to 2350 between late 1993 and late 1994, then streaks to around 8500 between 2006 and 2010.
- Oil prices drop toward $10 a barrel and even possibly lower by 1994 and stay relatively low for decades.
- Gold prices fall toward $200 an ounce by 1994 after rising temporarily in late 1992 or early 1993.
- The consumer price index drops 20 percent or more between 1992 and 1994, the biggest declines likely coming in 1993.
- 30-year U.S. Treasury bonds will rise toward 10 percent or higher in 1993, then fall to 4 to 5 percent between 1994 and mid-1998.
- Mortgage rates similarly fall to 5 to 6 percent by mid-1998.
- Average house prices drop by 20 percent or more by 1994 from their peak in 1989—with drastic drops of 30 to 60 percent in highly inflated markets like California—before prices start up again.
- Little or no inflation over the coming 20 years, despite dramatic economic growth.
- Japanese stocks fall and industrial power declines—the Nikkei Dow falling 80 to 90 percent by between 1993 and 1994 from 1989 highs.
- Japan's extremely overinflated $16 trillion real estate market follows stocks and collapses—the financial bubble burst of our time—causing a global real estate and banking crisis and leading to slower growth for Japan throughout the 1990s.
- A transfer of wealth to many Third World countries, particu-

larly Mexico and Eastern Europe, as they industrialize and
compete with the Far East for the subcontract production of
commodity products and components.
- The United States and the rest of North America—with Europe progressively moving into a close second position—regain
world economic dominance from the 1990s to 2010 and even
beyond.
- The next depression from around 2010 to 2025.

The implications for such predictions

This book has implications for readers in Europe, the former Soviet
bloc, Japan, and China as well as countries in North America and
Australia. Here are some of the benefits suggested and key mes-
sages to readers of *The Great Boom Ahead:*

Materially, an improved quality of life. Baby boomers will
be able to afford a higher standard of living than their parents.
This is the great fear of baby boomers—that they will be poorer
than their parents. The younger "baby bust" generation behind
them will do even better in this boom.
Disappearance of the "inflation tax." Baby boomers have
been paying an inflation tax for so long that it has been ingrained
into their standard of living and quality of life. We may see the
day when both spouses won't be forced to continue to work to
overcome the effect of this tax, as they have in the past to keep
their standard of living from falling. But I expect most families
will keep both earners in the work force, meaning higher earning
and spending capacities per family than in past booms.
Increased purchasing power. When the inflation tax goes
away, everybody will feel the immediate increase in purchasing
power. Baby boomers are going to be a rich generation in adulthood, able to afford the luxury car and the more expensive main
house in the suburbs or in smaller towns and cities.
Affordable housing. Lower interest rates and lower house

prices will fuel the boom in house building and buying—despite slowing household formations.

Changing markets and opportunities for business. Many products and services now in minority and niche positions in their industries will grow far more rapidly in the 1990s and early 2000s than they did in the 1970s and 1980s, moving into the mainstream. This means changing leadership in most industries, threatening many established products and services.

Wiser investment opportunities. Knowing the direction of the economy leads to more control and predictability in planning for retirement and college education for the children.

Improved employment opportunities. More jobs will open up with creative and entrepreneurial aspects to them. People sick of boring, rote assembly line and clerical jobs—which will be automated—will find more challenging opportunities in the new growth industries as business is reshaped to the demands of the more individualistic baby boom generation.

Changes in overall lifestyle. A general preference for safety, clean air, privacy, and selective intimacy—a kind of "humanness"—will lead a migration trend from suburbs toward smaller cities, towns, and neighborhoods similar to the last generation's move from the cities to the suburbs.

Preference for customization. The baby boom generation will demand more personalized, customized, high-quality products. These demands will move business away from production of standardized products on the assembly line to delivery of specialized, personalized products and services produced at the front lines of organizations as close to the customer as possible. New technologies will make customization more affordable for the average citizen—this will not be just a yuppie trend.

Greater leadership roles for women. New organizational and management trends favor the leadership tendencies of women, which are directed more at coaching and support and less at command and control. As baby boomers move into managerial power positions, more women will be there. A coming phase of the women's movement will be even more successful in making a positive statement on women's contributions to the economy.

The resurgence of America. The U.S. economy will lead the world in the boom. We boast the largest baby boom generation. Also, the trend toward customization favors U.S. businesses and skills. Our baby boom generation will produce the greatest economic and business effects. Canada and Mexico will join the United States as partners in a North American resurgence.

The reemergence of Europe. The fortunes of the European countries as economic powers are partially tied to the fortunes of the United States. But Europe will benefit in its own right from increasingly opening its markets although this will occur more slowly than has been forecast. Its smaller baby boom's spending wave will peak five to six years after the one in the United States. Europe will probably recover more slowly from this recession, due to a lengthier period of restructuring in Eastern Europe and the former Soviet Union.

Rising economic fortunes of the former Soviet Union. The post-USSR states will take longer to recover from the recession as they experience economic chaos. But these states will finally industrialize and grow with the rest of Europe, replacing Far Eastern countries as low-cost production subcontractors.

The emergence of China as a major economic power. The elements are in place for China to grow tremendously in the coming decades. By 2040, China will begin to emerge as a leading economic superpower.

The decline of Japan. After suffering the great financial bubble bursting of our times, Japan will see its own generation's spending wave peak between 1990 and 1997. The collapse of its enormous paper wealth and increasing protectionism will weaken its growth potential in the future. The Nikkei Dow and real estate markets will fall dramatically, if they haven't already by the time this book comes out.

A global depression. I'm forecasting a depression for the years after 2010 until about 2022 to 2025, bringing down the curtain on the greatest boom in history. Nobody wants to hear about another Great Depression, of course, but this forecast does allow you to prepare for and survive what I call (borrowing from an infamous Third World leader) the Mother of all Depressions.

Forget for a moment all the arguments you now have with my forecast and its implications. Shelve your doubts that anybody could make such a forecast about anything so complex as the economy. Instead of arguing and doubting, just consider a single possibility, however remote you believe it is. Ask yourself . . . *What if I'm right?* What would such a reliable forecast do for you?

I'll tell you what it would do. It would simplify your life.

You would be able to see more of the future than even the so-called economic experts. You would be able to make all types of business, investment, and personal decisions with greater certainty.

You would worry less about things you shouldn't have to be worrying about—like whether you were in the right business or whether you were making the right kinds of investments for your kids' education, or whether your business should be adding another store.

Businesspeople would know when to make investments in new capacity, marketing campaigns, and in hiring.

Consumers would know when to make investments in stocks, when to get into safer money market funds, when jobs will be easy or hard to come by, and what types of jobs will be available.

House buyers would know when to purchase or sell a house by anticipating the general direction of interest and mortgage rates.

You would be able to . . .

Take control of your own life

We live in an era of individualism in which the creativity and decisions of the individual supersede the old structures of managers, bureaucrats, and experts. Your career and business success will rely on your becoming the most powerful, creative force in your own life. This can be achieved by opening your eyes to the opportunities ahead.

Remember the very first words you read in this chapter? *Get ready!* You need this book to help you get ready for—even to survive—the coming boom well into the first decade of the next century. You need to know how to survive because this boom will be so dynamic and bring about dramatic competition between people seeking jobs, between businesses seeking to dominate markets, and between countries seeking to control world markets.

To take control of your own life. That's the promise I want to offer you in this book. Can it be done? You decide. Stay tuned. Prepare to have your eyes opened . . . and not by complicated economic mumbo jumbo, but by common sense and simplicity.

Now let's take a look at the Spending Wave, the most powerful predictive tool of all.

2

The Spending Wave

The driving force behind the economy

BULLETIN

We have tools that can rationally explain the recession of the early '90s. More importantly, we can pinpoint the recession's end coming by the second half of 1994! We can virtually see half a century into our economic future and even identify the basic turning points in the stock market.

Traditional economic forecasts

Forget for a moment every complex explanation you've ever heard for economic forecasting. Forget government management of interest rates. Forget import quotas. Forget the deficit. Unemployment statistics? The Dow? Business start-ups? Bank failures? The money supply? Forget them all. These things don't lead

the economy and they certainly don't drive it. They follow. So, by definition, *they cannot possibly be used to predict the economy—except in the shortest-term scenarios!*
So, what does drive the economy?

Consumers do! Your spending matters!

Traditional models simply don't work. Let's look at why.

The flawed Human Model of Forecasting

Study after study has proven that the experts as a whole don't predict the economy any better than random chance. Even with sophisticated computer models and detailed data, the experts still fall back on the tendency of human nature—to forecast by projecting trends in the same basic direction they are already going. This is shown by the Human Model of Forecasting, which shows that experts, despite their sophisticated tools, and the average person on the street fall victim to the same tendencies.

When you plot all the projections of the Human Model of Forecasting, you get a figure like Figure 2-1, full of arrows that fly off the curve of the actual direction of the economy. All but the shortest-term forecasts are often wrong unless a long-term trend keeps their conservative guesses close to the line by pure chance.

That's because, by nature, we tend to focus on present symptoms rather than root causes. This often leads us in the wrong direction. We also think and project in straight lines, although reality runs in cycles.

Refer to the model. At the left end of the curve, the economy

The Human Model of Forecasting

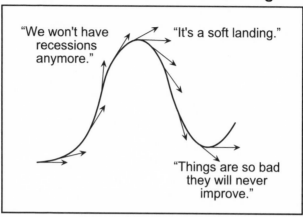

"We won't have recessions anymore."

"It's a soft landing."

"Things are so bad they will never improve."

Figure 2-1. How economic predictions fly off the mark

is level, so it's most natural to predict it will continue more or less on the same line.

When growth shoots upward, these level projections get left behind. As the markets and real growth climb, traders and fore-casters alike rarely can tell far in advance that a peak is near. Toward the top of every major economic boom, some leading experts will make statements like "We don't need to have recessions anymore. The Federal Reserve has found ways to fine-tune our economy." That's when the warning bells should start going off!

As humans, we're reluctant to accept down cycles. So we become overly optimistic when things in the economy are going well. It follows that we are reluctant to accept negatives.

So when the economy starts to flatten out, you hear predictions of a "soft landing." Remember the erroneous soft-landing forecasts in 1989 and the "no recession" forecasts for 1990? A national association of economists huddled and agreed there would be no recession for one to three years—they even announced their consensus publicly. Sure enough, a month later we were into it. And soon most economists and forecasters will think this recession is turning into a depression as they project a continuation of downward trends into the cellar—making statements like "Things can only get worse."

When the economy either takes off in a boom or dives into a bust, the economic experts almost always miss the turning points. The few who do catch the highs and lows are known as contrarians.

Finally, when we humans at last accept the negative, we tend to overreact with pessimism. We're reluctant to listen to good news because so much has been bad for so long.

Remember this Human Forecasting Model when we see the present mood of pessimism deepening in this country as the recession worsens, as it will just before things turn around. What is that mood? We hear it in statements like: "America can no longer compete in the world economy." "Today's baby boomers and young people don't have a strong work ethic and don't follow orders." "Our education system is deteriorating." "New technologies are sure to eliminate the jobs." From my contrarian point of view, such deep pessimism is actually a very bullish sign.

We need reliable, simple tools that counteract the human model and help us accurately forecast what will happen in the economy.

The powerful but simple driving force behind our economy

Consumers alone comprise 67 percent of the Gross National Product. If you include business capital spending in response to consumer demand, that percentage increases to almost 80 percent. The government is responsible for a little over 20 percent of our economy. But even that is derived entirely from revenue gained by taxing the income and profits of consumers and businesses. So the government does not drive the economy—it doesn't even drive itself—*we do*. That is, we fund the government with our taxes and we fuel the economy with our spending.

No matter how much we declare our free will and spontaneity, we are largely predictable animals. The economy is far more predictable than most of us assume because we consumers are highly predictable.

Insurance companies figured out long ago that people are predictable. That's why car insurance is more expensive for macho young men than for young women and for older adults.

Life insurance companies make money by predicting human mortality with a high degree of dependability. *These people know—on average—when you're going to die!* They know exactly how much they will have to pay out in benefits over time, and thus how much to charge in premiums to cover payouts and overhead and to leave something for profit and investments. If an insurance company gets into trouble, it isn't because their actuaries misforecast life expectancies and people start dying in droves. No, somebody got greedy and bought too many junk bonds with the company reserves.

No matter how complicated life insurance gets, it can be distilled down to a simple thing: average life expectancy.

With similar logic we can prove the economy is just as predictable as life insurance. Only here we're not talking about people dying. We're talking about the fully predictable ages at which consumers spend. We earn and spend at certain levels as we grow older. When large numbers of us earn and spend more, the economy responds with growth. When we will spend and the effect that it will have on the economy are just as predictable as when we will die.

This factor makes economics more like the actuarial sciences used in the life insurance industry. I call it . . .

THE SPENDING WAVE

Whether our economy booms or busts is determined by the earning and spending cycles of people as they age and raise families—and the effect of this Spending Wave on the economy is reliably predictable.

This principle is so simple it will make you wonder why we have debated the future of the economy for so many centuries. Too bad this logic is just too simple and straightforward for most economists.

Age 49—when family spending peaks

Economic boom periods occur as new generations of consumers progress up a predictable curve of earning and spending until they peak in spending between ages 45 and 49, more recently about 49. From 49 on, consumers begin spending less, especially on major durable goods like houses and furnishings, which causes a downward turn in the economy. Isn't it obvious what will happen when you have a huge generation of people growing up, starting families, buying houses, and spending more? Certainly. *The larger the numbers in a generation, the greater that generation's effect on the economy.*

How people earn and spend

Take a look at Figure 2-2. The U.S. Bureau of Labor Statistics conducts annual surveys of consumer expenditures—this graph is from the 1989 survey.

One look at the numbers and you can see why I say this is not rocket science. Kids younger than 20 don't make much money and what they spend is likely to be their parents'. After young people graduate, they start jobs and begin forming families, earning and spending more. They advance steadily in their skills and job responsibilities, moving toward that peak age. After age 49, they earn and spend less because their children have left the nest.

Now think about the implications for baby boomers. What you have is a generation of about 80 million people whose families will earn and spend more as they approach age 49. You can do some simple math yourself. What do you suppose is the effect on the economy when that happens? I say substantial.

Two factors account for the increasing earning and spending capacity of men and women in the work force. The first has to do with earning power. As people gain work experience, they advance

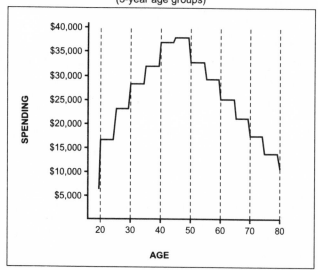

Average Family Spending by Age
(5-year age groups)

Figure 2-2. Spending for baby boomers peaks around age 45 to 49
Source: U.S. Bureau of Labor Statistics, Consumer Expenditures Survey, Interview Survey, 1989

in their responsibilities and earning capacities. The second, the family formation cycle, relates to spending. Between their early 20s and late 40s, the typical family is raising its children and building its stock of necessary household assets like housing, furnishings, and cars.

Purchases of durable goods from our 20s to our 40s, especially houses, furnishings, and cars, have the greatest effect on the economy. Why? These are major budget items that can be the most cyclical and volatile factors in our economy. For example, bank credit and the money supply expand and contract with the housing cycle. House purchases in particular create enormous financial leverage. So let's look at its effect in greater detail.

The most durable of goods— your house

When you buy a house, you typically put down 20 percent, and the bank creates the other 80 percent in the form of a mortgage. That's what I mean by leverage. And of course, a broad range of appliances, furnishings, and services concentrate around this major purchase.

During the early years, families buy cheaper "starter houses." Later, as the family grows, they move into their larger, more expensive "dream homes." Finally, after the kids are gone, it's increasingly likely that the parents, left with the empty nest, will move into smaller houses, apartments, or condos. Likewise, the number and value of purchases of autos will accelerate from the economy models to family cars and station wagons and kids' first cars. After the family has left home, the parents will likely have one last splurge for buying the luxury car they always wanted but put off for the sake of the kids.

Thereafter, parents no longer expand the family's durable assets like their house, furnishings, and cars. They don't need bigger houses and more cars. It's more likely that they will go on a maintenance and repair budget—replacing things as they wear out. If anything, they'll be downsizing the budget for many key purchases. Parents don't have to earn and spend as much once college is provided for. So they don't. And since many of their fixed costs like the mortgage are increasingly paid off, they have higher discretionary income for enjoying things like eating out and travel. Some work less, or work more part-time, or take less overtime. One spouse leaves the work force. Some people retire altogether in their 40s or 50s. People start saving more and spending less in preparation for full retirement.

In short, from age 49 on, people's reduced earning and spending habits shrink the economy, especially in the highly sensitive and leveraged basic durable goods industries.

What does this all mean to the economy? It means that the effect of the Spending Wave today can be seen by looking at birth rates of decades ago. The reason we can project the direction of the economy is that we know the patterns of people's spending habits as well as we know average life expectancies. People are born. As people age, they earn more. As they earn more, they spend more. Spending peaks around age 49, then it declines. That's the cycle. It begins, naturally enough, at birth, the origin of the Spending Wave.

The economy is predetermined
by the birth numbers

Figure 2-3 shows the cycles in births in the United States as far back as the numbers were recorded.

The last century has seen the formation of two generations of consumers. The largest by far is the tremendous baby boom of the '40s, '50s, and early '60s—about 80 million strong. It comprises more than two-thirds of our work force. By 1995 it will be three-

Birth Rates in This Century

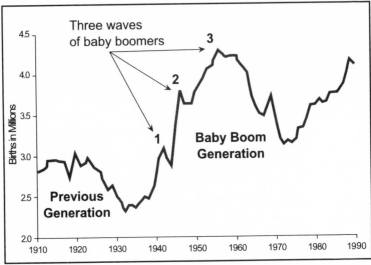

Figure 2-3. Cycles in U.S. birth rates.
Source: U.S. Census Bureau

quarters of the work force, where income and spending power is created.

That's all you need to construct a long-range prediction tool.

> You simply project the cycles of birth rates 49 years ahead when the generation is in its peak spending years.

Don't lay it down for the year people are born . . . newborns don't spend anything, right? And don't move it up 18 to 22 years, when young people move into the work force. Young people have no economic impact compared with people at their peak productivity. All an 18-year-old has is a few cases of beer and a cluttered apartment.

To test the Spending Wave all you have to do is project the birth rate from Figure 2-3 ahead 49 years for baby boomers, 47 years for the previous generation, and lay it down over the S&P 500 Index. What do you get? You get striking parallels between the two cycles, as shown in Figure 2-4.

The 47–49-year "Leading Indicator" applied to today's economy

Figure 2-4 shows how well this 47–49-year birth projection tracks with the general movements of our economy since 1956, using the S&P 500, adjusted for inflation, as a broad indicator of our economic health.

This indicator accurately forecasts the tops and bottoms of our economy within reasonable tolerances. It also picks up most of the recessions and growth surges in between. The Spending Wave indicates the timing of the boom of the '50s and '60s, precisely hitting the top in late 1968. It predicts the declining economy in the '70s as well. It shows the first wave of baby boomers beginning to drive the boom in the early '80s. The unprecedented debt accumulation of the '80s generated leverage that caused stocks to get ahead of the leading indicator.

Accounting for divergences between the indexes

A long-term indicator like the Spending Wave is not going to forecast random and political factors. It could not have told you the month of the stock market crash of 1987, but it could have told you that stocks were getting way overvalued. Just look where stocks went when the market crashed . . . right down toward the

The Spending Wave
The 49-Year Leading Indicator

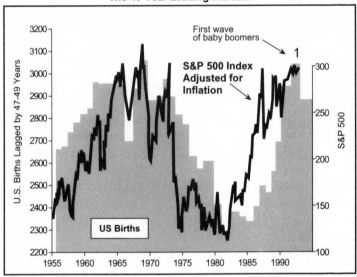

Figure 2-4. The historical effect of birth rates on the economy
47–49 years later

Note: Later marriages and childbirth have caused the peak in
spending to move forward. The birth projection is 47 years for
births in 1909–1921, 48 for 1922–1935 and 49 from 1936 on.

trend line established by the Spending Wave. It's clear to me that
the 1987 stock crash did not represent an economic downturn in
consumer and business spending. It was a result of overspeculation
in stocks and the sudden reversal of the government's policies on
interest rates from precipitously lowering them to letting them rise
aggressively. The rise in interest rates was necessitated by the
government's mushrooming trade and budget deficits, which first
put pressure on the U.S. dollar and then on interest rates to rise
to attract capital from overseas to finance the deficits.

But this is part of the beauty of this tool. Executives and managers could have known not to take that crash seriously in their business planning. Investors could have known that it was a shock that was likely to pass, not yet a sign of a stronger downturn. So this was not a time to panic and get out of the market during the crash.

Let's look at four divergences needing closer examination:

1958 to 1962—industrial overcapacity and shakeout
After the booming 1950s, America had an overcapacity situation in industry. So prices fell for a while as competition increased. Consumer buying continued up, but some company profits went down. Within four years that situation reconciled itself, so by 1965 the indexes fell exactly in line again.

1970—the recession This recession was a classic over-reaction to the overvaluation of stocks that is typical at the top of a long boom period when the market first realized it couldn't grow forever and corrected itself in a sharp downturn. Notice again how the market line soon stabilized and returned again to the basic trend line of the Spending Wave.

1973 to 1974—the first oil shocks You remember OPEC's effect on the global economy, don't you, when the Organization of Petroleum Exporting Countries decided to control the supply of oil to the West? The effect of that long-term divergence could not have been predicted by the Spending Wave. But after the first oil shock and the recession of 1973–1974, stocks rebounded right back to the trend line again.

1986 to 1987—stock speculation As I said, this crash was caused by aggressive Federal Reserve easing and then rising interest rates that followed. The stock market shot up, then crashed, returning overnight toward the line the Spending Wave would have predicted.

To me, the remarkable thing is not that these divergences occurred but that even when you don't account for them, there's such a striking and consistent tracking of the economy's performance with this single, simple indicator.

Next let's use the Spending Wave as a predictor.

Projecting the Spending Wave into the future

Now that I have shown you how the Spending Wave tracks with past performance of the economy, let's project it 49 years ahead.

The baby boom occurred in those three surges shown in Figure 2-3. The first surge drove the boom of the 1980s, hitting its peak in spending in late 1992. The recession will worsen into 1993 as this first wave turns down in its spending and the stimulative effect of election year fiscal policies wears off.

The projection tells us a lot. First, the recession will be over by late 1994, but only after the debt crisis takes stocks well below the trend line set by the leading indicator. I expect stocks to bottom between 1700 and 2350 on the Dow after peaking in late 1992. Second, when we come out of this recession the upturn will be dramatic. That's because the even larger second and third waves of baby boomers will drive the economy and the stock market to even greater heights for 12 to 16 years with a Dow peak of about 8500. So this next spending surge won't peak until around 2006 to 2010, when wave 3 is finished spending, with some potential choppiness between late 1996 and 1997 after wave 2 peaks.

You can see just how powerful the effect of the baby boom generation will be. Overall, the rise is steep and strong. The extended Spending Wave predicts an incredible peak of the stock market and shows the major turning points in the economy. That's the good news for the long term, of course.

However, the burst that follows the boom will be every bit as

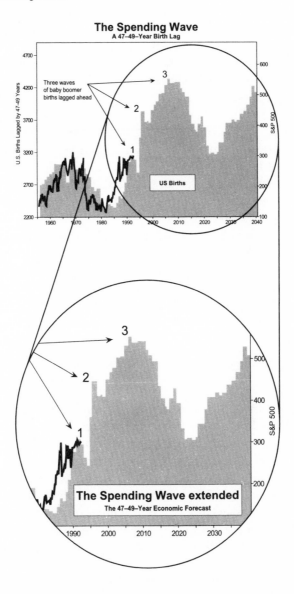

Figure 2-5. Projecting the Spending Wave 49 years ahead to predict the direction of the economy . . . upward until around 2010!

devastating as the upturn will be salutary—starting around 2010, when the height of the baby boom passes through its spending peak. That's when I predict the onset of the Mother of all Depressions—as opposed to the multitude of forecasts for the Great Depression of the 1990s.

How long will the depression last? Twelve to 15 years. Why? The peak of baby boom births occurred between 1957 and 1961. The next wave of births did not turn up until 1973 to 1976, or 12 to 15 years later. So you can expect a major economic downturn starting around 2010 and lasting to around 2022 to 2025. No amount of government stimulus will prevent it, just as it didn't prevent the Great Depression of the 1930s.

There you have it, a forecast for the basic direction of the economy into the next century.

The bottom line? This tool works. You can use the Spending Wave to peg the economy 49 years into the future. What more lead time could you ask for?

Refining the Spending Wave

Of course, spending is more complicated than the 49-year indicator shows. Housing is the key factor in the economy, especially where recessions are concerned. The most concentrated surge of spending in a family's life cycle comes as it approaches age 43, when most of us buy our largest house and all the furnishings that go with it. House buying then drops off as consumers approach the spending peak around age 49 and then drops off dramatically. And remember, housing is also the most leveraged purchase we make as banks create 80 percent of the purchasing power through mortgages.

Although the commonly accepted definition of the baby boom generation is the above-average birth years in the stretch from 1946 to 1964, the important factors in economic terms are the rising and falling tides of births in any generation. These tides cause the economy to boom and bust predictably. From my perspective, births were rising from 1933 until 1961, when they peaked, and turned down again. Within this 1933–1961 birth boom, there were those three concentrated surges in births that most affect spending in the coming boom, particularly housing.

These surges are shown in the first column of Figure 2-6. I project them ahead 43 years in the second column. This figure will give you an idea of when the most concentrated periods of spending will occur in house buying and therefore expansion in bank and credit cycles.

Look at the effect that first wave's peak housing surge from late 1982 to 1986 had on the economy. Peak spending from mid- to late 1982 to 1986 was the most dynamic part of the 1980s. But we experienced a one-quarter recession in late 1986 and the stock crash of 1987 following this first surge.

From late 1988 to 1990, despite building debt pressure, the second surge kept the economy going until the recession set in during July of 1990.

Birth Wave Surge	43-Year Housing Peak
1 — 1939–1943	late 1982–1986
2 — 1945–1947	late 1988–1990
3 — 1950–1957	late 1993–2000

Figure 2-6. Table of baby boomer spending peaks for housing

Right here is where we can get the best picture of why we've been
in a recession since late 1990. As the table shows, there's been a
void in the demand for housing between the second surge of baby
boomers peaking in late 1990 and the third, much larger surge, which
will begin in late 1993. This weak demand and falling house prices
have been the chief causes of this recession and the key reason we
as consumers have been so pessimistic. From late 1992 to 1994 the
first wave's downturn in overall spending will aggravate recessionary
pressures further. With both indicators down in 1993, expect 1993
to be the worst year in this recession scenario. We all have built up
a lot of debt buying our houses in the '70s and '80s because of
inflationary pressures. But we never expected our house prices and
equity, which supported that debt, to fall. Of course, neither did the
banks!

Based on this refinement, I forecast that housing will be the first
sector to begin to lead us out of the recession. Therefore, I do
not expect any signs of a significant recovery until at least late
1993, and it will more likely not occur fully until mid-to-late 1994
due to the impact of the first wave's decline in spending into 1994,
government tinkering to stave off the recession in 1991 and 1992,
and extenuating world events throughout this recession. The greatest concentration in spending on housing will occur between late
1993 and late in the year 2000.

So, in summary, our 49-year Leading Indicator shows us how
the boom that started in the early '80s will go much higher beginning in 1994 and not peak until 2006 to 2010. The 43-year housing wave within the Spending Wave allows us to see both the
times of greatest spending growth and the times of greatest vulnerability to recessions. The greatest growth should occur from
1994 to 2000 and the greatest vulnerability to recession will be in
1993.

Finally, a couple of thoughts about this idea of "Age Wave
Economics." I often hear two good questions: Doesn't productiv-

ity peak later than age 49? And isn't there a trend toward living longer?

True, most people don't peak in their productivity at 49, but as a rule, they spend less from around 49 on—because they choose to work less. There's also a trend toward living longer. But this trend has not seemed to change the mid-life peak in spending much. Later ages for marrying and having kids seem to explain the advance in the peak from age 47 in the past to age 49 for the baby boomers. The fact that more people are living longer will have a mixed effect, in that many people will also work longer but many people will also require government and family support longer.

In the main, the peak in spending for the last century has stayed between around age 47 and 49, so I'm sticking to 49 for the baby boom as a working figure until I see evidence to suggest that the peak is moving further forward.

Can the Spending Wave explain the Roaring Twenties and the Great Depression?

Yes. Our Spending Wave model shows a strong correlation between the Leading Indicator and the performance of the economy in the Roaring Twenties and the Great Depression.

But because the government didn't keep year-to-year birth statistics before 1909, I have had to estimate births after the Civil War based on generation cycles outlined in *Generations.*

What emerges from this refinement of the Spending Wave is Figure 2-7, which shows that the boom of the 1920s and the downturn in the economy that persisted throughout the '30s and '40s was just as predictable as the boom of the '50s and '60s, the downturn in the '70s, and our present boom period.

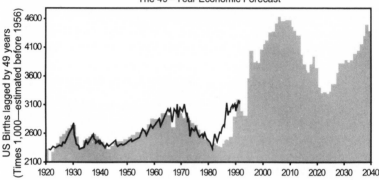

Figure 2-7. The Spending Wave extended back to 1920 using
estimated birth trends

What else can we learn from
the family life cycle?

The implications of the family life cycle go beyond tracing spending
and the general trends in financial markets.

Increased savings   Figure 2-8 shows how savings rates will
predictably go up as baby boomers age. Young people have to
borrow to get off the ground with their mortgages, car loans, and

screaming kids. But older people save more. There are two concentrated savings phases in the family life cycle, ages 35 to 44 and
50 to 74. Baby boomers will be moving strongly into this first range
from the early 1990s into the early 2000s. Results? As savings
increase, there will be more capital for our economy to invest
without our having to rely on Germany or Japan. This means a
lower cost of capital for our businesses, which will make them
more competitive and help encourage a longer-term view on capital
investment again.

Labor shortages out to the year 2015   One reason Japan's
economy has shown higher productivity than ours is they've already

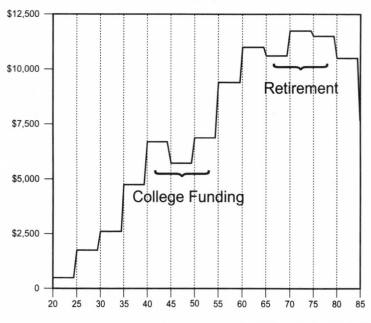

Total Family Checking, Savings, Securities
By Age

Figure 2-8. Savings patterns of Americans
Source: U.S. Bureau of Labor Statistics, Consumer Expenditures Survey,
Interview Survey, 1989

encountered an aging work force and realized they had to automate
many jobs. Their older population had the savings and productivity
to finance it. Automation causes higher productivity as well. The
United States will have to invest in automation in the future, especially in the clerical and low-skilled entry-level jobs because there
won't be people who will take them.

Figure 2-9 shows the shrinking growth of the labor force.

The conclusions from this graph are quite simple. Our economy
will experience dramatic growth while our labor force hardly grows
at all—less than 1 percent a year for most of the coming two
decades. This means we'll have to produce more per person. In
fact, our productivity will have to nearly double by the end of this
boom. That's in high contrast to our recent past when we had
teenagers coming into the work force willing to work for $4.00 an
hour. Would anybody make big investments in automation under
those circumstances? No. Too much risk, too much investment—

Figure 2-9. The shrinking growth rate of our labor force
Source: Paine Webber, *The Renaissance of Growth*

they just hired the young people. That luxury will be disappearing
for the period of this boom.

So what's left? The obvious . . .

Increased automation
Will automation really happen? Yes.
Our people will be at the same stage as the Japanese were ten
years ago. Because they will be saving more, money will be there
when cheap labor isn't. Our own productivity growth levels will be
more like those of the Japanese in past decades. So we will automate more and more. Not because of some superhuman insight.
And not because American management is so smart—although it
is rapidly becoming smarter. Not even because we feel the competitive pressure from the Japanese. Few people act decisively just
because they're smart. They more typically do things when conditions force them into action.

And we will be forced to automate. Because we will be saving
and investing more money as an aging society, we won't be obliged
to borrow the money from Japan, which may not have it anyhow.
Good things are going to happen to us in spite of ourselves, but
this time our automation will be driven more by investments in
flexible software systems rather than the standardized hardware
machinery of the past. These investments will make our jobs more
human and more creative as well as higher-skilled and higher-paid.
But the bottom line is that we will see the beginning of a great
white-collar automation trend, as we saw in factory and farm jobs
in the past. More than 70 percent of our work force is now involved
in systematic clerical and white-collar work, which computers can
do faster, better, and cheaper.

Nothing matters as much as
the Spending Wave

What about the other factors presumed to affect the economy?
What about the money supply? Interest rates? The stock mar-

ket? What do all these things have to do with cycles in the economy?

These factors do have an effect on the economy, usually a short-term and self-correcting effect. Remember this—if you reduce interest rates and increase money availability, you don't increase people's purchasing power or earnings. You only make it a little easier for people to borrow. People who borrow more today retrench their spending tomorrow as the debt service catches up with them. To put it in simplest terms: If you borrow the money today, you have to pay it back with interest tomorrow, so there's no free lunch. Recent history has clearly proven—as in 1986 to 1987—that when the Federal Reserve pushes interest rates down for a time, there's a clear tendency for rates to rise in the period afterward. Purchasing power is only substantially changed with changes in age and experience, technology, and organizations. As to the stock market, it is only a short-term indicator that reads and reacts to indicators like interest rates and money supply. It often reads the long-term direction of the economy rather poorly. And when it's wrong, it crashes.

Can any tool forecast the economy beyond 2000?

Before you get excessively enamored of the Spending Wave as an economic forecasting tool, I should say what it is and what it is not.

First, what it is: The Spending Wave is a tool that can be used—decades in advance—to predict the general direction and level of consumer spending that is going to come as a generation grows up.

Second, what it is not: The Spending Wave does not predict oil shocks; it doesn't predict the effects of government tinkering with the economy and sharp changes in interest rates; it doesn't predict wars against the armies of Saddam Hussein. Where I can, I have pointed out the extra effects of unpredicted events because, in the short term, oil shocks, wars, and government fiddling with interest rate policies do rearrange the normal patterns a little.

Mind you, immediately after the easing of the oil shock, the stock market went right back down to where the Spending Wave predicted it would be. After the 1987 crash, the Spending Wave corrected the stock market back to where it would have gone.

In summary, this tool is something you can use to predict long-term directions in the economy. You'll never be able to predict world events, but you can know enough to see what an anomaly the 1987 crash was—why stocks were getting increasingly over-valued and why once they crashed it would be a temporary phenomenon.

One final point to emphasize here is that, although the Spending Wave is a central factor, it is just one wave of three successive waves. The Generation Wave of baby boomers will bring into its striking growth and maturity entirely new waves of technology and social and organizational changes every bit as revolutionary as the economic changes I've talked about.

It is difficult to overstate the influence of the baby boom generation, already responsible for a clear majority of spending in our economy. By 1995, it will also become 75 percent of our work force. This means that many product trends, management trends, business trends, and social trends of baby boomers will accelerate as their spending power and dominance of the work force increase. Just as that generation begins to flex its muscles as it gains leadership in the work force, in management, and in government, the United States will reassert its own leadership in global business and technology.

Brighten up, America!

There's more to our future than merely a booming economy. We're about to enter a modern era of automation and productivity—this time in the white-collar sectors, from clerical workers to professionals and managers.

The greatest advantage the United States will enjoy in this era originates in our strong creative skills and in our entrepreneurial sectors—the very strengths of our baby boomers. This generation is spearheading an entrepreneurial revolution going mainstream, leading toward an individualized, customized economy. That is the direction in which the United States is headed. And where we go, the rest of the world must follow.

Right now everybody has a negative attitude about the economy. Baby boomers are jaded because their high expectations have been unmet. Given our occasional urban unrest and difficulties with drugs, education, and unemployment, many minority advocates don't feel sanguine about the economy. And with good reason. Frankly, many people will have a hard time measuring up to the requirements of an economic boom. They won't be equipped to handle the upward mobility and so will be at risk of being left behind.

On the other hand, we'll have intense labor shortages at a time of economic growth. These shortages will give businesses incentives to train or retrain these lagging sectors and to bring them into the fold. In the main, the boom I'm predicting will raise the standard of living for most people and reduce unemployment and social costs.

So no matter how dismal the view now, things are going to turn the other way once we realize the gifts to come from the real investments, sacrifices, and changes we've made in the last twenty years. Believe it—the recession of 1990–1994 is going to be as memorable as yesterday's hangnail. In fact, it will be a blessing in disguise.

The blessing I'm talking about is the subject of the next chapter—the end of inflation.

3

The Purchasing Power Dividend

*The end to inflation means a
new era of prosperity*

BULLETIN

The pain of inflation is about to go away. In fact, this boom will mark the virtual end of inflation for many decades to come. Your purchasing power is about to take a leap forward. Interest rates will drop. Prices will drop. The economy as we know it is about to enter a new era of affluence!

When I speak to groups about the greatest boom in history, nobody listens indifferently. People react. Their responses range from hopeful skepticism to scornful disbelief.

Most people just can't accept the promise of good news in my forecast after experiencing inflation and low productivity for so long. The prevalent line of incredulity runs something like this: "Well, this baby boomer thing is fine but we're living in a new time." And: "This generation is not going to earn what their parents earned." Or: "How can we expect progress with a defective educational system and poor SATs?" And more typically: "Baby boomers as a generation are declining in productivity. Foreign workers are outdoing us . . . So how can you assume the spending and earning line will go upward as it has in the past?" And always: "What about inflation? As soon as things start to improve, prices will shoot up, and inflation will come roaring back."

Inflation, the great bugaboo. Everybody expects inflation to be the dragon rearing its ugly head to terrorize consumers and businesses. Most people assume good times must necessarily be accompanied by a dose of a new evil. The very mention of inflation is usually followed by a chorus of "amens" and remarks like "All bets are off. Things have changed."

My answer to that is: "Yes, things *have* changed, and it's about time!" We'll see an enormous difference between the '80s and '90s, a difference expressed in two words—*purchasing power*. The baby boomers, as well as the rest of us, have been fighting inflation for twenty years. In effect, they have been paying an extra tax.

No more. In this boom, the dragon will be slain.

Say goodbye to the inflation tax

Besides the burden of city, county, state, and federal income taxes, sales taxes, and social security taxes, we have been paying anywhere from 5 to 20 percent as an inflation tax over our adult lives. That 5 to 20 percent tax on everything we buy has pushed us into debt and forced us to have two-income families just to keep up.

The inflation tax especially unnerves baby boomers. Not only have they paid more for their houses, but interest rates have been higher because of inflation, sending up the cost of buying anything on time. Being the first credit card generation, did they ever buy on time!

Baby boomers have been hurting for a long time, and many of them don't even know the cause of their distress. So I can imagine how hard it is for them to believe the pain of inflation is about to go away altogether. But it is.

> *It's very likely that we'll see a period of negative inflation—or de-flation—which means prices will actually drop.* In the coming years we will see inflation going from 5 percent into rare negative territory. The consumer price level should drop substantially for the first time since the 1930s—a likely 20 percent or more.

The most surprising and critical aspect of the coming boom— and the most influential factor in making the boom the greatest in history—is that purchasing power is about to take a leap forward just as we enter an era of unparalleled productivity.

Picture this . . . interest rates drop, prices of goods—from canned corn to houses—come down, oil prices fall. All of a sudden baby boomers find purchasing power they never dreamed of. Their dispositions will change utterly. They will think differently about the size of the house they can buy and the type of neighborhood they can live in, the type of convenience services they can afford. Everybody would like to be able to enjoy a weekly maid and a lawn service, but they've been saying, "We just can't afford that now (or ever)."

People can't imagine how in ten years the average person in this country might be buying a house that costs $150,000 to $200,000 today and owning a luxury car in the Lexus or Legend class. It's going to happen.

When I ask people about their financial fears, they say, "I can't afford to live in a good house like my parents."

There you have it—the greatest anxiety of all for baby boomers, and I suppose for all generations. People don't fear this impersonal thing called inflation as much as they fear the possibility that they will have a lesser standard of living than their parents. That, it seems, is the measure by which successive generations judge personal failure.

Never fear. Baby boomers will be buying houses even better than their parents'. The $150,000 house of today may soon cost in the range of $120,000. Mortgage rates will fall to 5 to 6 percent by early 1998. Remember, productivity and real incomes will grow much faster during the boom.

> *Removal of the inflation tax is going to be a rocket launcher setting off economic recovery.* It will ignite spending as consumers begin to appreciate their new wealth. That catalyst, combined with the baby boom's Spending Wave, already in place, will propel our economy into the greatest boom in history.

I realize this thinking goes against the grain of conventional wisdom. Remember the Human Model of Forecasting from Chapter 2? Don't make the mistake of those economists who predict more of the same. Don't try to take a flat economy and extend it into the future. Just because you've fought inflation for twenty years and it's been hard for you to afford a house doesn't mean that will be true ten years from now. Things go in cycles, remember? Above all, don't believe those doomsayers who are trying to sell you the notion of so many similarities between the 1920s and the 1980s, suggesting that another Great Depression will follow. That's false. If anything, the tendencies of today are more *dissimilar* to the period before the Great Depression!

Stick with me on this, and I'll tell you how inflation works. Then I'll tell you how the end of inflation is going to work for you.

Normally economists will not predict a dramatic recovery following a period of lengthy sluggishness in the economy. They see debt everywhere in consumer, business, and federal sectors. They see the housing market slowing. They see plunging car sales and an overall stagnant economy. Everybody has the opinion that there's just no way we can grow, except slowly.

That's wrong. We're going to scream out of this recession.

Forecasting tools that promise the coming new prosperity

Any number of existing tools can be used to predict inflationary periods with varying degrees of accuracy. We all know that high oil and other commodity prices had a lot to do with causing inflation in the '70s. We know that our government deficits and higher defense spending of the last twenty years have been big factors in inflation. We all know that the accumulation of debt, especially in the '80s, by the government, consumers, and corporations has been driving inflation.

And all those factors do have a bearing on inflation. In fact, they now form an impressive array of evidence to back up my assertion that inflation has ended for the baby boom generation. I discuss each of them with you as I build my case for the end of inflation.

But the central driving factor is not any of those. It is, again, the baby boom generation. I've already shown how a single key indicator, the Spending Wave, can drive the economy. I'm about to tell you of an astonishing predictive tool that—by itself—proves to be the key explanation for inflation in the baby boom era.

The key factor driving inflation   The single factor driving inflation is the baby boom generation's rate of entry into the labor force. Remember Figure 2-9 from Chapter 2? It shows the rate of growth of the labor force. In researching this book, I discovered an astonishing relationship between labor force growth rates and inflation rates.

Figure 3-1 shows that labor force growth correlates with inflation better than any other factor—and I have studied them all! The lower productivity and high investments required to incorporate such a generation peak about three years after entry into the work force. That's why I lagged the labor force growth three years.

What this chart would have predicted if it had been available

Figure 3-1. Baby Boomers entering the labor force—a tool that predicts prices will continue to stay low throughout the coming boom

earlier would have been a peak of inflation in 1980—which occurred—and a first period of deflation from 1980 to 1986—precisely in line with the labor force growth inflation indicator. Inflation came down from over 20 percent in 1980 to as low as 3 percent in 1986. And then after 1986, an almost perfect reflection of the indicator would have told us that inflation would rise modestly into 1990 followed by a second deflationary period from about 1990 to 1997.

To me this is a mind-boggling relationship, as much a breakthrough chart as the Spending Wave. Many factors explain inflation, but if you examined nothing but the rate of baby boomers coming into the labor force, it would be an astounding predictor.

Why does this work as a predictor?

If we get beyond the commonly accepted idea that government deficits are the sole driver of inflation, we can learn something.

First of all, we've had very high government deficits during deflationary and even depressionary periods like the 1930s, so there's no direct, carved-in-stone relationship between deficits and inflation.

> I simply define inflation as the economy's means of financing a period of high investment. In other words, inflation occurs in our economy in any period in which there is a high requirement for investment and low productivity or savings and profits to finance it. The economy simply borrows from itself or its own consumers by raising the prices of goods and services.

The first thing you'll notice in history is that inflation tends to accompany periods of war. That's simple to explain. You have a high investment to fight the war and low productivity because few people are available back home to produce goods and services. More than that, wars typically occur during changeovers in technologies, shifting the balance of power, with new powers often having to fight the old powers for supremacy.

So periods of inflation most commonly occur during transitions between old and new technologies when we see low productivity from the peaking of the old technologies and industries. We also see the need for investment to retool old industries and to launch new ones.

As we hinted in Chapter 1, technological innovation and transition periods occur when a generation is moving out of the school system into the work force in their late teens and early 20s.

But along with technological innovation, the actual entry of a generation into a work force similarly causes both a high requirement for investment and a period of low productivity.

Why would there be low productivity?

When eighty million young, inexperienced baby boomers moved into the job force in a relatively short period, do you even have to ask? Young people are not as productive as more experienced, older workers. A high percentage of young people in the economy means increasing chaos and revolution—not high productivity!

The entry of many young people into the work force requires high investment. People need training. They need office space. They need desks, computers, and other equipment to do their jobs. Lester Thurow has calculated that it requires an average investment of $245,000 per child to raise them and to initially incorporate them into the work force. Quite an investment indeed!

And they need time to get a bit of experience under their belts. Almost all managers have had the challenge of giving young workers new assignments and projects and holding their breath, knowing the high risk of failure. But effective managers know they must be willing to make the investment in a young person's learning curve. This willingness often requires costly trial and error, but it also nearly always pays off in the long term in higher productivity and bolstered confidence as young people mature. We must understand that our young workers are investments that pay dividends in the future.

Another factor related to reduced productivity and high investment is the rate of savings. People in their late teens and early 20s have the lowest rates of savings. So there is less capital available for companies to fund this high level of investment.

As with the Spending Wave, the larger the generation, the higher the inflation rate—we've just experienced perhaps the greatest rate of inflation in history brought on by the sheer size of the largest generation incorporated into our work force as they brought an unprecedented wave of powerful new technologies.

So if you agree with my conclusion that the sheer numbers of baby boomers played the leading role in causing inflation because they required an enormous investment at a time of low productivity, what's your next conclusion? That's right—baby boomers will guarantee the end of inflation because they no longer need that investment to sustain them. On the contrary, they will be highly productive as they move into their 30s and 40s, with a much higher rate of savings to boot.

In the last twenty years we have incorporated unprecedented numbers of baby boomers into the work force, along with radical new technologies and information infrastructures. We'll reap our dividends in the next two decades. And huge dividends at that!

What other forces work in favor of the purchasing power dividend?

Crank in a multiplying factor for women. Our inflation and our work force growth were so high, not just because the baby boom was huge, but because women were entering the work force in large numbers for the first time in history. In the past, Japan and, to a lesser degree, Germany had the advantages of older, more productive work forces, higher savings, and low labor force growth and investment—resulting in higher productivity and lower inflation.

> In the future, the United States will achieve the highest productivity because we had the biggest baby boom and we incorporated a high percentage of women and minorities into the work force. Not only do we have the largest work force heading into their productive years, we have the greatest proportion of two-income families, which means double the earning power and productivity compared to past generations. Because of our minority mix, we also have the most international work force for attacking global targets.

If there is going to be inflation anywhere in the world in the coming years, it will be in Germany, where high investment will be required at first to incorporate lower-productivity East Germans and other Eastern European workers into the economy.

Factor in another item. Every trend I can measure shows labor force growth slowing dramatically following the peak of the baby boom. That means we don't have to build so many new offices and install equipment around people. Basic training costs will also go down.

Forget about that pervasive gloom about a lack of productivity, an inability to compete in world markets, permanent inflation, and a recession that will last forever. The fundamentals of inflation say all these trends will be reversed. We're coming into a time when we're going to be more productive. We're not going to be fighting this inflation monster in the future new era of prosperity.

What about all the other causes of inflation?

Before we go into predicting the detailed effects of deflation on our economy in the coming years, let's go into all the other causes and indicators of inflation. You will see that all indicators correlate—although none as strongly or as consistently as labor force growth rates. But they all point in the same direction, toward the end of inflation.

Falling commodity prices   The first and most potent stage of our most recent inflationary period occurred in the '70s. The primary driver of it was not the Vietnam War spending but the enormous rise in commodity prices led by the great explosion in oil prices up to $40 a barrel.

If we look at the commodity prices in Figure 3-2, we can clearly see they peaked in 1980 and have been trending downward ever since. They will continue to move downward as new technologies reduce the amount of energy and raw materials needed to produce products and growth in our economy. In fact, the great scarcities of the '60s and '70s have developed into increasing surpluses in the '80s and '90s.

If OPEC hadn't restricted oil production, we would already have a huge glut. Now Russia is showing an inclination to dump commodities like gold and oil on world markets to raise money for economic survival. Eastern Europe and the new independent former Soviet states will also be increasing agricultural outputs over time. So from a global perspective, we can reliably foresee a continuing slide in those commodity prices over the long haul.

In this country, the very success of our old technologies and industries in saturating our economy with many different products in the '60s and '70s, ranging from autos to canned foods, created strains on our natural resource base and on our infrastructures. We drove more miles. We demanded larger, more powerful automobiles. We wanted more houses and more appliances. This, not the federal budget deficit, created scarcities and allowed OPEC to raise its prices, holding us hostage to petroleum products for a while.

All raw materials became more costly as they grew scarce.

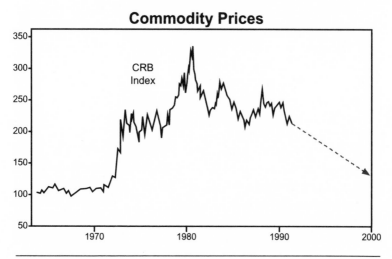

Figure 3-2. Phase I of inflation: the 1970s commodity price explosion

Either we had to dig deeper for them at higher costs or import them from farther away. Add to this the increasing costs of pollution and safety regulations caused by high levels of production and consumption in the old industrial economy.

Growth always comes up against limits. The more our economy and technologies succeed in making things cheaper and more available, the more it strains the natural resource base. The limits to the last cycle were classic—so many cars and so many appliances using so much oil and steel that we simply started running out of short-term resources. The first step in inflation is a commodity price explosion like that beginning in the early '70s and peaking in 1980. Oil price increases eventually drove up prices of iron ore and other commodities that require petroleum consumption. Then all other heavy industries that depend on oil and other raw materials saw their cost of doing business shoot up. On top of all that, our manufacturing-based economy polluted the environment.

However, new technologies won't rely on huge amounts of raw materials manufactured with heavy machinery fueled by oil or coal. Instead they will be fueled by information and run on microprocessors, which are much more energy-efficient.

Commodity prices are coming down because these new technologies are working against them.

Can commodity prices be counted upon to predict inflation? Hardly. If they alone had been driving inflation, we wouldn't have had it since 1980, when prices tailed off. We can't depend on this indicator as the sole factor responsible for inflation. So let's look at another important component, shown in Figure 3-3.

Shrinking debt accumulation   When commodity prices fell, debt accumulation accelerated, causing a continued inflation in the 80s. The rate of debt accumulation peaked in 1986 and has been heading down sharply ever since.

Look at Figure 3-4 to see the ratio of our country's total debt to the gross national product. It looks serious enough to write your congressman. But, contrary to popular opinion, the federal government isn't the only sector of our economy that borrows heavily

Rate of Debt Growth

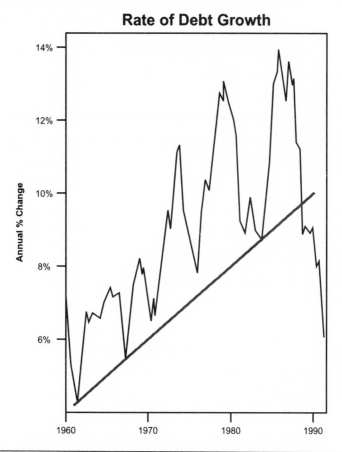

Figure 3-3. Rate of total financial debt growth in the United
States
Source: BCA Publications Ltd., 3463 Peel St., Montreal, Canada

and runs huge deficits. Businesses and consumers have accumulated debt to almost the same relative degree as the government.
In fact, only about $4 trillion of the estimated $16 trillion debt in
our economy belongs to government. That's roughly proportional
to their 20 percent-plus spending share. Consumers and businesses
account for the other 75 percent of the debt, about $12 trillion. If

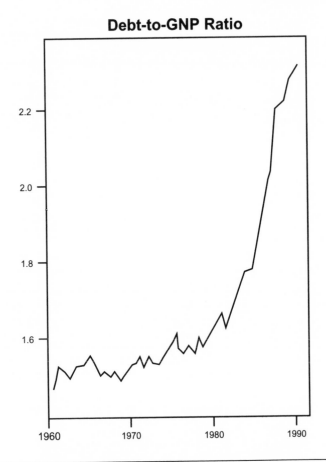

Debt-to-GNP Ratio

Figure 3-4. Phase 2 of Inflation: The Debt Explosion
Source: BCA Publications Ltd., 3463 Peel St., Montreal, Canada

we're having a debt crisis in this country, it is far more due to consumers and businesses excessively borrowing than to government.

We've all heard about leveraged corporate buyouts, but the growth in consumer mortgages to finance inflated housing prices has been the greatest debt factor in our economy. Excessive credit card debt is the other significant cause of consumer debt growth.

The reason the government deficit is so noticeable—besides the

fact that we always like to point the finger at somebody else—is
that the government uses accounting methods that differ from those
of consumers and businesses. The government expenses even
long-term items totally in the year of expenditure. That means
government is on a cash-in/cash-out budget. Businesses amortize
major investments like new plants and offices and heavy equipment
over decades. So the government will show a cash flow deficit
while a business can be borrowing more and still show a profit.

What would happen if government used the same accounting
methods as business? Robert Eisner, president of the American
Economic Association, found that by taking the government's
budget, amortizing long-term investments, and lumping in all state
and local surpluses and deficits, the then highly touted $150 billion
deficit turned into a $70 billion surplus! So don't be too alarmed
by the federal deficit. And if you don't like the idea of giving credit
to government for boom times, it hardly makes sense to lay economic hard times at the federal feet.

We consumers amortize our biggest expenses too. For example,
our homes are usually amortized over the term of a 30-year mortgage. The upshot of all these trends is that debt as a percentage
of GNP went up slowly in the '70s and then skyrocketed in the
'80s.

When the economy and profits are down, and productivity is low
for consumers, people have no way to keep up with their needs
except by borrowing. As long as there's more debt, more money
chases assets—banks lend more and more money so consumers
can buy houses, which drives house prices up. There's more debt
in California, for example, because banks will lend more money on
a house than they will in Ohio. That's why California's housing
market is likely to crash much further. That's what drives the
housing market up, for instance. If banks didn't lend the money,
prices would never go up, thus adding to the debt spiral. Remember
what happened to the price of United Airlines stock in October
1989 when the banks simply reversed their decision to back that
leveraged buyout proposition? The stock dropped from $300 to
$100 in a week. That's how the availability of debt drives the prices
of assets up or down.

The predicted effects of debt accumulation and its reversal   For the short term we're going to have unprecedented government deficits. I wouldn't be surprised to see a deficit of at least $800 billion to $900-billion-plus occurring by 1994. This is a perfect example of how the government's own deficits will drive interest rates up on the heels of its efforts to drive them down in 1991 and 1992.

After the recession, interest rates will drop, and business will grow. During the recession, defense spending will be cut faster than originally planned, generating government savings far into the future. As the economy booms again, unemployment and other related social spending will come down and, more important, government tax revenues will rise dramatically because consumer incomes and business profits will be on the rise. Then the government deficit will reverse itself. Governments run deficits during inflationary periods and surpluses during the booms that follow—this has been the case throughout history. Remember, things go in cycles.

After those enormous deficits in 1993 and 1994, government will start to wind down federal deficits and will probably be in a surplus situation by 1998.

In summary, in the '80s the accumulation of debt pushed inflation strongly, just as commodity prices drove inflation in the '70s.

But debt, like commodity prices, is now in a downturn. That's just one more reason to expect deflation in the future, not inflation.

Less defense spending   Defense spending has been the greatest source of government deficit spending. As you know, this spending remained high in the '70s and '80s in the Cold War arms race. Governments always face major military conflicts and defense buildups during inflationary periods. Inflation represents a time when economic power is altered among nations due to changing technologies that shift the balance of power. Wars tend to be the way in which such changes in power are tested and proven— declining powers rarely give in to the new without a fight. World War I and the Civil War occurred during our last two inflationary periods. So did the Cold War, with its largest military buildup in history during the most recent inflation cycle. In the Cold War, we in effect spent as much as if we had fought a major war.

With the collapse of the Soviet Union, defense spending as a percentage of GNP has peaked. It will be declining even as we have to continue to police the Saddam Husseins of the world.

The fact that baby boomers will not have to pay as much for defense in the future means that purchasing power will be freed up. Formerly, baby boomers were being taxed for defense, not only through direct income taxes but by the indirect tax of inflation.

The three-year cycle in interest rates   Interest rates are really just a symptom of inflation, but they affect our lives just as much as inflation rates.

I haven't yet found the precise reasons, but I have observed that interest rates have followed a consistent three-year peaking pattern during the 1980s and early 1990s. Rates climbed to peaks previously in 1981, 1984, 1987, 1990, and now 1993. The stock market has experienced mild (1984) or sharp (1987) corrections every time this three-year cycle has caused interest rates to peak temporarily.

Such a consistent cycle cannot be guaranteed to reoccur, but we ought to consider it until we see otherwise. We are making a lot of bold predictions already!

Just as interest rates peaked in late 1981 coming into the recession of 1982, and came down dramatically in the years to follow, I predict they will rise into the recession of 1993 and come down rapidly from 1994 on, although we may see a brief rise against this downward trend in 1996 due to this three-year cycle. Lower interest rates themselves will have a deflationary effect on the economy.

My best forecast: A substantial drop in interest rates between 1994 and 1995 and a more dramatic drop between 1997 and 1998.

The presidential election cycle   Another cycle in the economy worth noting has been in effect far longer than the three-year cycle in interest rates. There's a four-year presidential cycle in stocks. The two years before a presidential election, stocks and the economy tend to be up, and in the year or two after an election a significant intermediate correction usually occurs. So we have historically seen short-term bottoms in stocks in 1962, 1966, 1970, 1974, 1978, 1982, 1986, and 1990. These temporary lows result from the fallout of election pump-priming policies of two years earlier as the incumbent tried to ensure his reelection. And don't put the blame only on politicians. We voters sent a message to President Bush in 1991 and 1992: "Give us a pill to cure this sick economy or you won't get reelected." He did, and now we'll experience the consequences in 1993 and likely into 1994, no matter who is elected.

This cycle calls for corrections in 1994, 1998, 2002, and 2006. These can be minor or major. If the stock market bottoms in 1993, we may see a small correction in 1994. If we have a limp recovery or stall in 1993 and the recovery is not over, we could see the bottom between May and November 1994. My best guess for the bottom in stocks would be around October 1994. But I expect the worst of the crash to occur in the first half of 1993.

The cycle in 2002, if it is still active then, could be significant because a three-year interest cycle falls in the same year, following the third wave of baby boomers peaking in house buying. This could cause this cycle to generate a short-term correction in stock prices—maybe even something like the crash of 1987. But stock prices should rise to new highs from 2002 into 2006 to 2010.

The deflation scenario— a forecast for the '90s

Not only does our primary indicator show it, but all basic inflation-generation factors appear to be heading down in the future. Clearly, the future holds lower prices, not a renewal of inflationary pressures—even despite the stimulative effects of the preelection policies and practices of the Federal Reserve.

In Figure 3-5 you can examine the first phase of deflation from 1980 to 1986, which resembles many other deflationary periods of history that I've studied, to get a clear picture of what happens to the economy in a deflationary period.

When inflation comes down, it causes recessionary pressures from the inevitable shakeout in business. At lower prices inefficient businesses that have been propped up by inflation for a long time

The 1980s Bowl Cycle of Deflation

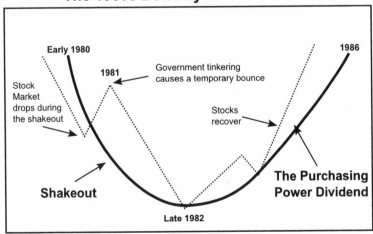

Figure 3-5. The Bowl Cycle shows how the deflation scenario works

can no longer make a profit and compete. Businesses fold. People lose jobs. Between 1980 and 1982 we had an on-and-off recession with bouts of rebounding as the government stimulated the economy to keep it out of recession to no avail.

In 1980 we went into a recession. The government stimulated the economy, bringing us out into 1981. But by the last part of 1981 into the fall of 1982, the economy fell back into a deeper recession with stronger deflationary pressures and 10 percent unemployment.

Based on this, the inflation rate went from over 20 percent coming into 1980 down to 3 percent at the end of 1982. The unemployment rate went up to 10 percent as many businesses couldn't stand the pressure. Then we experienced a dividend, the positive phase of deflation after the recession of 1982. Interest rates dropped on a 30-year government bond from 14 percent down to 7.8 percent, with mortgages following. A much lower rate of inflation meant less of an inflation tax for consumers to fight. So consumer purchasing power was much stronger after 1982 than it was in the '70s.

Our age demographics from Chapter 2 showed there should have been a particularly strong surge in house buying and spending by the first wave of baby boomers between late 1982 and late 1986. It was the confluence of falling interest and low inflation rates combined with age-driven spending that caused the explosive economic growth of the 1980s, particularly the steepest surge between 1982 and 1986.

The same dynamics will play even stronger in the '90s, as shown in Figure 3-6.

From late 1990 through 1991 we fell into a recession. As in the earlier recession, the government has tried to stimulate us out of it. So we got a rebound in 1992, but only a very mild one, with stock prices rising. I expect the greatest amount of deflation to come after the election, as in 1982, when the economy went into a deeper plunge. So look for stocks to fall sharply from late 1992 or early 1993 into mid-1993. The period of greatest vulnerability being from February to June 1993. But that crisis will set the stage

The 1990s Bowl Cycle of Deflation

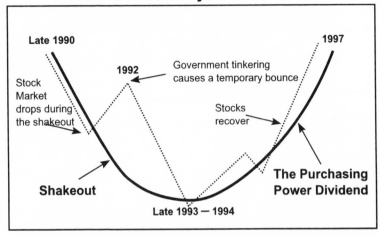

Figure 3-6. The 1990s Bowl Cycle with the current deflation scenario at work

for the end of inflation and lower prices and interest rates from there on, creating the purchasing power dividend for consumers. But this time we will have a much larger and longer wave of baby boomers moving into their peak house buying and spending. That's why I have said this terrible recession will be seen as a blessing.

At the earliest from late 1993, or at the latest from mid-to-late 1994 on, interest rates will again be falling dramatically. My forecast is that the 30-year government bond will go toward 10 percent-plus in 1993 and then in 1994 start falling toward 4 to 5 percent by late 1997 or mid-1998. Mortgage rates will follow, falling to 5 to 6 percent. As I said earlier, I expect the inflation rate will fall from about 5 percent in 1990 into a negative rate of inflation, or an actual deflation of consumer prices. Consumer prices will drop significantly for the first time since the 1930s—as much as 20 percent or more.

A higher standard of living—twice the house for the astute buyer

You never expected it, but in the years to come you're going to be able to afford a lot!

Let me give you an example of the purchasing power dividend. Take your house, the most expensive, price-sensitive purchase in most people's lives. This recession will bring down the prices of housing 20 percent or more, on average. (House prices will rise again with the recovery but probably more slowly than in the past.) If a $150,000 house goes down to $120,000 and you can ultimately finance it at mortgage rates of 5 to 6 percent, that means that on the same salary you can afford roughly double the house. What could be more bullish for the economy than that? As in 1982, housing will be one of the strongest components leading us out of this recession, counteracting many of the other negative factors that tend to keep the economy sluggish. The loss in equity during the recession by most families who own homes will be more than offset by the lower prices and mortgage rates of buying a much larger trade-up home in the years to come.

Despite bankruptcies and failures and unemployment and government deficits, people with jobs will start finding house bargains. The first people to buy will be those who have been complaining because they couldn't afford a house. These people will have an advantage. Those who didn't buy before won't have declining equity positions. They won't have a bad balance sheet. They will be in the best position with banks to borrow.

How this recession will finally unfold—
the Chapter 11 economy

As the economy weakens in 1993, we're very likely to see the unexpected component of deflation: prices actually dropping in many areas rather than just a decline in the inflation rate. This is when the recession's real chaos will be unleashed, going beyond the government's ability to control it. With falling prices, industries from oil producers to automakers to house builders to services will see weaker competitors going under. This will cause a banking crisis as mortgage and business loan defaults rise rapidly. The result: a temporary Chapter 11 economy. Banks and businesses in many industries will see a restructuring of their assets and debt. Stronger competitors will assume the assets of weaker competitors, while banks and other creditors have to take write-offs in the debts these businesses owe them.

This will be a very painful process that will result in high temporary unemployment levels, probably 12 to 14 percent. The greatest levels of unemployment and layoffs are likely to come from the service and government sectors, as they are far more overstaffed and unproductive than the manufacturing and agricultural sectors of our economy that had already experienced significant deflation and shakeout in the 1980s. California will be one of the worst-hit economies in the nation due to its overinflated real estate and high proportion of service and defense industries. The great era of migration to California is clearly over for now. The result will be a much more efficient and competitive business and banking system, much lower prices for consumers, and a lower debt burden for consumers and businesses.

Can we be sure we won't see
another Great Depression?

Some of you still have questions, like "How can I be sure it's not really the next Great Depression?" Others will ask, "How—with all the obviously negative patterns—could this last phase of the recession be over so quickly?" Your fears will be heightened by gloomy economic predictions amidst the Chapter 11 economy.

Because of the great accumulation of debt and because we will see prices fall for the first time since the 1930s, many economists will take it as the final sign that we are in another Great Depression period. They will be dead wrong!

About the time they've convinced everybody of disaster is when we will roar out of this recession with falling interest rates and unprecedented consumer spending. Contrary to most people's opinion, change and restructuring in such a deflationary recession can happen very quickly. This is because when there is a crisis, resistance to change disappears in the face of survival needs.

Let's take a look at some history that demonstrates how quickly these depression fears can turn around.

Many great deflations have occurred within one to two years. We've already shown that the worst part of the 1980–1982 recession was over in less than a year's time, between late 1981 and mid- to late 1982. That's one lesson from history that demonstrates a deflationary recession can end abruptly just as conditions seem to be at their worst. Here's another lesson.

History lesson   Everybody from the Bob Hope generation remembers the Great Depression. Because that generation never tired of telling about it, baby boomers know about the crash of the stock market and the extended period of joblessness and deflation and depressed prices. But did you know that even the worst of that was over within three years?

And hardly anybody remembers the time between 1913 and 1920. That's when the country saw inflation spike up during a long-term recession in stock prices. This was followed by the growth boom of the Roaring Twenties, ending with the Great Depression. Figure 3-7 shows the pattern of the wholesale price index.

Notice the deflation in prices that followed inflation in 1920 to 1921. Wholesale prices dropped 35 percent in less than a year. Consumer prices fell 20 percent, and commodity prices plunged 50 percent or more. You don't hear many economists talk about the huge deflation of 1921—although we experienced a greater relative degree of deflation than that of the Great Depression. I think the general silence exists because nobody has ever really understood it.

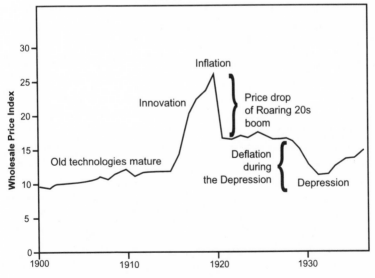

Figure 3-7. Actual performance of wholesale prices (inflation track) during the early 1900s

From late 1919 on, we had a mild downturn that only turned into a sharp deflation and recession from late 1920 into mid-1921. The worst of that crisis also happened in less than a year's time—with unemployment levels quickly reaching 11 percent. Then we roared into the 1920s—the greatest boom in history to that time. We're coming into a similar deflationary period. Although such a deflation will temporarily deepen our current recession, it will also lay the foundation for a prosperous boom for consumers and the noncommodity business sectors of our economy by creating lower debt, lower prices, and lower interest rates.

Does this resemblance prove anything? Is the economy preordained to experience an exact repetition of the Roaring Twenties? Of course there is no absolute guarantee, but all the indicators support it. We had a period of inflation with the innovations of the Henry Ford generation and World War I, and we had one with the innovations of the baby boom generation and the Cold War. Surprise, surprise! Will we experience another, more pleasant surprise with a huge drop in inflation? Depend on it.

Because of the similarities to the Roaring Twenties, we almost called this book *The Roaring '90s*—and the main reason we didn't was that it wouldn't encompass the boom accurately. The true boom period doesn't lend itself to a title of *The Roaring '90s and Early 2000s*. Yes, I fully expect the pattern of the '20s to be repeated in the '90s and beyond—but on a larger scale.

So it's not necessarily true that once deflation sets into an economy it is a sign that you must be on the verge of a prolonged period of depression. One other critical factor must come into play to trigger a depression. In the '30s we saw a long lull in consumer spending patterns between two major generations. It extended through the '30s and the '40s. That's what caused the protracted period of depression then.

I have predicted the Mother of all Depressions to come after the baby boom generation peaks in spending about 2010. But for now, a prolonged depression simply isn't in the cards for the United States.

With that notion set aside, let's look at the '90s scenario.

The longer-term economic forecast
for the United States

Here's a forecast of the U.S. economy for 1993 and beyond.

We've already established that the boom of the '80s was driven by the first wave of baby boomers entering their peak spending years and the first wave of deflation dividends. My best forecasting tools tell me that at the very earliest in the second half of 1993, probably in the summer or fall, we could begin to pull out of this recession. This prediction is based on the likelihood of a resurgence in consumer spending on housing.

The cycles I have studied in stocks suggest that the most likely month for the first bounce in stock prices—and stock prices tend to lead the economy in times of turnaround—would be June 1993.

However, the first wave's downturn in overall spending should continue to impact the economy into 1994. Also, given the uncertain effects of government tinkering and outright bungling of this recession in financial terms and strong influences from mega-events in overseas markets, I'm suggesting it is more likely we won't see a bottom and a sustainable recovery until mid-to-late 1994. May 1994 is the first potential turning point. Stocks should bottom at the latest by the fall of 1994.

The more severe the Japanese financial collapse (see Chapter 4, "The Tidal Wave from Tokyo") and violent outbreaks of unrest in areas like the former Soviet Union, the higher the odds the turnaround could occur well into 1994.

Stock prices should surge strongly coming out of this recession. The market may be a little more cautious at first than the bond markets. Stocks have been slammed in 1987, 1990, and now in 1993, so traders could remain wary for a while.

> Stocks should bottom between 1700 and 2350 between the summer of 1993 at the very earliest and mid-to-late 1994. But more likely in mid-to-late 1994. They will likely surge back toward new highs again by late 1996.

My complete rundown on this forecast is in Chapter 8.

As I've said, the recovery will be strong. If we see a feeble recovery in the second half of 1993, I won't be convinced that it's the real McCoy. As in late 1982 and as in the deflationary recession of 1921, which set off the Roaring Twenties, the recovery should be strong, not like the cautious bounce of 1992. The bounce our housing indicator predicts in late 1993 may be mitigated by high interest rates. A weak bounce in 1993 would likely mean a postponement of the recovery until 1994. When it happens, we'll come roaring out of the recession. It will be clear and strong. We will remember this time as the Roaring '90s.

> My best forecast for the peak in interest rates is for the second half of 1993. This coincides with that dependable pattern of three-year cycles in interest rates since the early '80s. Then rates will drop dramatically between 1994 and 1998, with the strongest drops occurring in two periods, between 1994 and 1995 and 1997 and 1998. Why? The three-year cycle suggests a temporary rise of rates again in 1996 before heading down in 1997 or so. A 10-year government bond ought to drop from 10 percent-plus down to 4 to 5 percent. Mortgage rates will drop from 11 to 12 percent or so down to 5 or 6 percent.

Remember the four-year presidential cycle? In 2002 it could be significant because a three-year interest cycle hits it in the same year, and the third wave of baby boomers peaking in house buying could intensify it into a short-term correction.

From 2002 on, consumer spending and productivity will remain relatively buoyant until 2006 or 2010, when the baby boom cycle comes to completion. The strongest surge of baby boom spending and house buying will be finished by late 2000 or 2001.

> I expect the economy to continue growing until at least 2006 and stay relatively buoyant until 2010.

The bottom line on the new era of prosperity

I've tried to show you that inflation is not some random form of government thuggery brought on when a maniacal politician comes to power. Inflation happens when new technologies and new generations cause a restructuring of our economy across the board. Periods of high innovation require inflation, deficits, and borrowing. They are times of great entrepreneurship and radical innovation, out of which emerges the greatest leaps in economic growth and in our standard of living. Why? Because we make great investments—albeit financed by inflation—investments that, if made in the right technologies and industries, will pay off handsomely in the future. Hey, inflation is beautiful if you understand it (and if you can gut it out).

Durable goods producers will benefit from lower costs and lower financing rates as consumers, already poised to buy based on baby boom demographics, will buy more major items.

Businesses as a rule will see their profit margins rise. That's due to lower costs from deflation and the progress of new technologies coupled with a corresponding rise in consumer demand that will ease the pressure of having to cut prices to sell.

The best of all times are those that follow periods of high inflation. In fact, history will show that the greater the level of inflation, the greater the boom to follow. We have just witnessed the greatest inflation in history, and therefore we should see the greatest boom in history. We're now heading for a short, difficult deflationary period to be followed by a strong boom that will be characterized by relatively stable prices and an absence of inflationary pressures. How could this be?

It is simply a matter of supply and demand. The progress of our new technologies will continue to put downward pressure on prices, but that downward pressure will be countered and balanced by the upward pressure that rising consumer demand will generate. This will result in stable prices but higher profits and margins for businesses—which means greater wage gains for workers.

Those are the clearest insights I can derive from putting together the dynamics of the Spending Wave and the factors affecting inflation. Everything points to prosperity. But as remarkably positive as this outlook is, even further signs point to a boom, and a strong resurgence of America.

To understand how businesses will change and grow and how competition will improve in this period of the greatest boom in history, we have to look at the Innovation Wave in Chapter 5— because, as I said in Chapter 1, the innovations of the past two decades will now move into the mainstream economy, bringing high levels of productivity and causing huge changes in market and business leadership during the boom.

But before we look at the causes and nature of that boom, we have to examine something considerably less palatable—how Japan's collapse will heighten and trigger this deflationary crisis, greatly affecting the United States and world economies in 1993 and beyond.

4

The Tidal Wave from Tokyo

The collapse of Japan's money machine aggravates the global recession into 1993

BULLETIN

We will eventually see a New World Economic Order in the coming decades. But before this World Economic Order takes shape, there will necessarily be a worsening of the current recessionary shakeout, led by a series of calamities originating in Japan.

Inevitable Japanese economic calamity

Most of us have praised Japan for its collaboration between business and government. That tight relationship has often been the subject of open envy in our country. At times I've heard our business and political leaders clamor for the same thing on the home front. But the excessive collaboration between Japanese business and government is actually going to be seen as their Achilles' heel during 1993 and 1994.

What's the one important economic lesson the world has learned from the Communist experiment of Eastern Europe, the former Soviet Union, and countries like Cuba in the last couple of decades? *Centralized economies do not work as well as market-based economies—particularly in an age that makes information more accessible to everyone.*

Few countries have been able to prove otherwise. Yes, Germany centralizes successfully to some degree. And Japan seemed to have been the economy that achieved the exception. The Japanese have been extremely successful in their central planning, enjoying spectacular growth, leading in many aspects of the global economy in the last decade.

"Wait," you say, "Japan isn't a centralized economy. Japanese industries and government merely collaborate."

Not true. Japan's economy is highly centrally planned, and its society is still basically a feudal one run on fear. It is not at all a free-market system. No free-market system would have allowed real estate and stock prices to reach the absurd levels of recent years in Japan.

To exaggerate only a little, the excessive collaboration between government and business in Japan is far more analogous to the Mafia than to a free-market economy. The Japanese have rigged their economy from the top down, creating a financial engine and revving it to run at 7000 rpm, and even the best high-performance engines can't run at 7000 rpm forever.

Japan's entire economic underpinnings will inevitably collapse, creating the financial bubble burst of our times.

Japanese stock markets and real estate markets were the most overvalued in the world at the time of this writing. Price-earnings ratios reached 60 and higher on the Nikkei Dow in late 1989, making them the most overvalued stocks in the world. That's nothing compared to Japanese real estate. It has been valued at about $16 trillion, greater than all the real estate in the United States and twice the value of all the stock markets in the world! Need I say more? It won't be the stock crash alone that causes the crisis from Tokyo. It will be Japan's real estate crash that will create global deflation and deepen the worldwide recession. As of August 1992, Japanese stocks have already crashed 65 percent. Real estate has only dropped about 20 percent. Stocks will crash further to 5 to 20 percent of their peak values. Real estate will finally drop to 20 to 40 percent of its peak values. If this hasn't begun by the time this book comes out, we're certain to see a more severe real estate crash begin in Tokyo in 1993 when large amounts of real estate–backed debt financing comes up for renewal.

How could this happen? How could values be so overinflated in the first place? Answering those two questions is the purpose of this chapter. I'll show you how Japan has rigged its economy to benefit during times of inflation. And I'll demonstrate how, as the inflation cycle is ending, giving way to deflation, the Japanese are going to be the great losers in the global recession. I'll tell you how the aftershocks of the Japanese collapse will create a global tidal wave, actually worsening that recession for a time—but creating huge competitive opportunities in the future for the United States, Europe, and Third World countries like Mexico.

The bubble is about to burst

Every 400 years or so we've seen a great period of technological innovation and structural change that has been accompanied by high inflation. At the end of every cycle, we've seen a speculative financial bubble burst. The last example was the dramatic rise and fall of Spain in the 1500s and 1600s, where we saw high inflation following innovations like the printing press, gunpowder, and the discovery of the New World.

This concentration of the collapse in Japan by 1993 will mark the end of a current cycle of innovation and inflation. Next comes the bursting bubble—Japan's great wealth will evaporate far faster than that of any other country in the world. The Japanese won't recover for a long time. So they won't be a heavyweight contender in the coming boom. They simply will not be the economic superpower that they were in the past, leaving room for the United States to emerge as the clear economic leader, much as the collapse of the former USSR almost overnight allowed the United States to re-emerge as the clear military superpower.

Japan's money machine

The Japanese created their wealth through the collaboration among their government, industry, and business. They have created the great money machine of our time. It has been instrumental in fueling high asset prices, the ability to expand industries, and to change over to new technologies at a rapid rate.

This is not to say this process was an evil proposition. Quite the contrary. The world needed such a money machine to finance a huge social and technological restructuring even though it led to an extraordinary period of inflation. We created a monetary, debt, and real estate bubble in our own economy. Michael Milken was a key player in the United States with the innovation of junk bonds and leveraged buyouts. But he was a peanut vendor compared to the Japanese.

The greatest inflationary periods in our history have always been followed by the greatest booms. The problem is that they have also always produced financial panics in the short term.

Good or bad, let's look at the combination of strategy and circumstance that allowed the Japanese to create their money machine.

The trade surplus   The first strategy of the Japanese economy was to generate a trade surplus. They used aggressive export

strategies, focusing capital and government priorities on support-ing key industries. These were largely standardized hardware products, at which they excelled because of their marvelous pro-duction process technologies and solid management and engineer-ing skills. They competed fiercely. But they cheated too. They protected their home markets against imports to help create a surplus.

That strategy accumulated cash from other countries—mainly the United States—and they used that capital to invest all over the world.

Artificial interest rates   In addition to the high flow of savings from consumers, the government did its part to keep interest rates artificially low. So Japanese business enjoyed a low cost of capital. Companies were able to invest and to raise money cheaply. That's one reason Japanese businesses were able to surpass the rest of the world in investment and take a longer-term view in their in-vestment strategies.

On the downside, it also led Japan into investments and industries with low profits and low rates of return—which in a free-market economy signals decline and longer-term unattractiveness. As Ja-pan's economy has become more integrated into the world econ-omy, Japan has increasingly lost its power to control interest rates at home. So rates have been rising. And the Central Bank of Japan has been forced to tighten its monetary policies to choke off the speculative bubble in real estate.

Cross-investment   Japanese economic collaboration encour-ages cross-investment and collaboration between government and businesses and among businesses. This is another way to keep cash flow and asset values high among Japanese businesses. More important, it prevents free-market decisions. It protects busi-nesses from the natural pressures of the marketplace—like the corporate raiders that forced U.S. businesses to restructure into more efficient business units. Does anybody want to raid a Japanese company at 60 to 80 price-earnings ratios? No way!

Working terrible—the sacrifice of smaller businesses

The Japanese economy operates far differently from how most Americans would guess. Japan is not a nation where the majority of the work force is employed by the multinational corporations like Sony and Toyota. On the contrary. Something like 76 percent of Japan's work force is comprised of small family businesses.

People in these smaller Japanese businesses are expected to sacrifice, breaking their backs for the large, export-oriented companies. They work terrible hours under terrible conditions, only to earn minimal profits. Why? To provide low-cost subcontracted components and services to the large companies like Sony and Toyota. The large Japanese companies' greatest advantage is not merely their size or economies of scale—it is their highly efficient and flexible subcontracting network of small businesses that are something akin to sweatshops. They sacrifice out of national loyalty and, of course, fear!

People in small business in Japan have been asked or forced to sacrifice profits and margins and standard of living for the good of the country—which bases its success on its large export-oriented conglomerates. Result? More profits and, hence, capital to invest. But the Japanese people, as they travel, see the better standards of living—especially in housing—of consumers abroad and are increasingly less willing to make such sacrifices. This is especially true of the younger generation.

A strategy of entering cash cow industries

What did the Japanese do with the capital generated by these strategies? They invested in mature, hardware-oriented, standardized industries to gain global market share. When you gain market share in mature industries you create what is known as a cash cow. Mature industries throw off profits as cash, unlike most emerging industries that only require more investment above profits to grow and stay in the game. The Japanese took the cash flow from those industries and reinvested it—creating even more cash. And where do you suppose it went?

You got it. The cycle perpetuated itself.

The cash went back into the effort to create even more market share and more cash flow that could be reinvested again. Naturally, this cycle made the Japanese continually stronger and better able to invest globally even as they were earning no or low profits— as long as the Japanese businesses were able to continue to gain market share and cash flow. But what happens when the ability to gain market share slows due to rising competition and protectionism? The game ends—and you have a lot of unprofitable and overvalued companies! As you might expect, the cycle leads to other consequences we'll discuss later.

The Generation Wave edge of the past
Japan's equivalent of our baby boom generation is older than ours. So it moved into its Spending Wave boom in the '70s. Members of that generation enjoyed their more productive years while our baby boomers were in high school and college and were very unproductive. Meanwhile we were in the declining years of the Spending Wave of an older generation.

So in the '70s and in the '80s Japan had a more productive, higher-spending, higher-saving work force. Incidentally, the Japanese savings ethic comes from basic fear and insecurity. Most Japanese people, especially that 76 percent in small businesses, do not have pension plans or social security. The Japanese, in part, work so hard and save so much because they're afraid of retirement. The Japanese may show somewhat of a greater propensity to save than U.S. citizens, but comparisons that normally suggest that their savings rates are more like 20 percent and ours are 5 percent are misleading. Most of us, like it or not, have forced savings of 16 percent for social security, when both employer and employee contributions are considered. So this is savings and does provide capital for the government to allocate. The truth is, we also save 20 percent when social security and other savings are combined.

Whatever reasons, increased savings in Japan meant increased capital available for lending and investing.

Let me summarize to here. The Japanese launched export-oriented industries in their own strong home markets, which are protected from foreign competition. Later, they attacked the rest of the world in mature hard-goods industries with their economies of scale and efficiencies to compete with our industries in our home markets. We often see that as an industry miracle. However, it doesn't look so miraculous when we see how leveraged their system is and how that leverage is getting ready to be reversed like an overstretched rubber band. And I haven't yet addressed the most influential factor of all . . .

The House of Paper   Probably the most critical aspect of the Japanese money machine is their accounting system, which generates paper profits to drive it.

In Japan, the value of assets—company stocks, pension funds, investments, capital machinery, real estate and buildings—is calculated annually at current market value. This is an accounting practice not used in American companies, where assets are simply and conservatively valued at cost, adjusted for depreciation.

This means that Japanese balance sheets grow not only because of greater investments and profits but also because of inflation. And in Japan, due to their highly rigged marketplace, the inflation in stock and real estate values has been far more extreme than here. These annual rises in asset values translate directly to the bottom line as paper profits. Now that's a highly leveraged method of accounting. Such a market-value accounting system allows a company to leverage inflation just as a mortgage leverages the investment in an American home. You only put 20 percent down on your home. With inflation, it goes up in value as fast as or faster than inflation. So you have a leveraged hedge against inflation.

The Japanese system works because the more inflation in assets, the more their assets and profits go up in value. That's how real estate and stocks got to such extremes. The higher these valuations, the more profits and assets they show. Which means they can borrow and invest more.

All of these factors, but particularly the market-value accounting system, explain how the Japanese have amassed capital. To stay competitive, to have the latest technology, to gain market share, and to be aggressive in marketing—again, even if it was marginally profitable or unprofitable to do so—they reinvested that capital faster than any other country in the world. Their goal, as Lester Thurow states, was to build empires and power—not profits and wealth. It's been a good strategy. It has succeeded. We've all watched in awe as the Japanese miracle materialized in the '70s and '80s. But . . .

The Japanese strategy of growth paradoxically was not very profitable. Returns on their investments have been very low on average compared to countries like the United States. Therefore, their growth has not been sustained by profits or real wealth, but by the growth of their money machine itself. Yes, they have pursued an empire—not wealth and profits. But empires historically have tended to overextend themselves and disappear rapidly and dramatically.

There's a catch to the money machine

Since Japanese businesses are so highly leveraged to take advantage of inflation and to create paper cash and paper profits, they are vulnerable. A number of factors will bring on an economic upheaval. Japanese wealth will evaporate faster than that of any other country in the world. I don't think they will fully recover from such a strong blow for many years. Watch for Japan to suffer worst and to be the last major country to recover from the global recession. Their economy could be dragging behind for ten to fifteen years. That's because so many factors have come into play at the same time, compounding the impact of the blows against the country's economy. Let's look at some of those factors.

The great equalizer—deflation   What has already begun, and is certain to continue in our world economy, is the trend toward deflation.

We saw in Chapter 3 how the rate of inflation peaked in 1980. I made the case that inflation will end in the present deflationary cycle. The Japanese scenario works fine as long as there is inflation. But guess who will be the biggest losers when their assets stop climbing in value? The Japanese, of course. Since they were the money machine for the world, they necessarily bought most of the overvalued assets at the top of the inflationary spiral. Remember the Van Gogh art at $86 million and Pebble Beach at $800 million? These were just the newsworthy signs of what was happening to a much greater extent elsewhere. They spent countless billions buying companies and real estate around the world. They built plants everywhere at the cost of many more billions. They invested heavily in Third World countries. They bought at least one of everything at the overvalued prices their money machine helped to create.

And now . . .

Now, when the deflation cycle inevitably hits—and deflation has followed every other period of inflation in history, so you can bank on this happening—Japan will suffer crushing losses.

Overvalued assets   Only a system highly rigged to allow excessive collaboration between government and industry would permit PE ratios on stocks to get into the 60-plus range. The PE is the price-earnings ratio, a measuring stick that tells how much the price of the stock exceeds earnings. A PE ratio of ten when you buy a stock indicates you're paying ten times over the stock's earnings. You pay this price with the expectation that the stock will earn back the excess, either in dividends or in appreciation.

Our free-market system rarely allows our stock markets to go much over 20 in PE ratios. When they do, we get a crash as in 1987 and the crash I'm predicting for 1993, which brings values down to reality. As I said, Japanese stocks hit PEs of 60 and higher in late 1989. Japanese stocks at that top were worth far more than all the stock markets of the United States combined. Now, that is inconceivable. Obviously they were overvalued. Even in late 1992, PE ratios were in the 35 to 45 range after the stock market had already collapsed 60 percent or more.

But as I warned earlier, the greater danger comes from the more overvalued Japanese real estate markets, which were worth five to six times what their stock market was.

So the collaborative system that set out to generate higher market values so the Japanese could surpass the rest of the world in investment depended on inflation.

But inflation is over.

Every one of the tools Japan used to build its advantage is reversing. Interest rates are climbing after years of holding them down. Other countries around the world are reacting to Japan's protectionist policies, demanding that the trade surplus be shrunk. Let's not be cruel, but realistic. Stocks, real estate, and even Van Goghs are retreating in value around the world. Now, instead of paper profits, Japan will be experiencing the reverse leverage of paper losses in declining assets. Without the ability to keep expanding market share, and without rising asset values, the money machine stops. When it stops, Japan's miracle comes to a quick and dramatic end.

The Japanese are going to suffer the financial crash of all time, and much of the sympathy you will hear will be hollow platitudes masking the sound of wicked snickering.

The Tidal Wave from Tokyo

The effect of a crash on Japanese market-value accounting will result in more than a simple reversal. As the global economy moves through the recession, not only will Japan's operating profits be slowed, they will get hit by devaluing real estate and stock prices. That's a double hit because losses will be leveraged in the opposite direction of profits. Since their stocks and real estate are so overvalued, you can expect an imploding bubble.

We've seen such things happen in pockets of the United States—

from the effect of the oil industry bust in Texas to real estate collapses in Arizona, in the Northeast, and to some extent in California. We've seen an even more dramatic example in our stock market crash of 1989, which centered not so much in the Dow Jones as on the transportation index due to leveraged buyouts in the airline industry. A leveraged buyout, like the market-value accounting system, uses high amounts of debt to allow employee and management groups to buy their companies' stock with little cash down. But in late 1989 banks finally decided they were not going to provide the loans to support these buyouts. It wasn't a prudent risk. Remember, overnight the market value of United Airlines stock went from $300 a share down to around $100. That's how fast asset values and a money machine backed by debt can deflate.

That kind of dramatic correction is what I see happening in Japan. The Japanese are simply not going to have the wealth and capital they had. Think about the average worker who might have a nest egg sunk into these overinflated stocks and real estate. After the crash, the consumer economy will contract. Their businesses will have to stop investing overseas—in fact, they'll even be forced to start selling investments abroad to protect their more critical assets at home.

Inevitably, this crisis will back up to Japanese banks. When the banks start bailing out, you're going to see real estate follow Japanese stocks right down the tube. If it hasn't already occurred by the time this book is published, expect the severe drop of Japanese real estate to send a tidal-wave shock across the Pacific.

Picture this scenario. Real estate values drop into a black hole in Tokyo. Panic explodes outward, forming the tidal wave. The Japanese stop investing in foreign real estate and even start selling some properties overseas to protect their domestic holdings. That means the markets of Hawaii will be utterly bashed soon after Tokyo's. Hawaii's home markets and vacation properties are the most overvalued markets left in the United States. Vacation properties are the first to go belly-up in a recession because they are considered luxuries and people will sell them off when money gets tight.

The tidal wave then rolls onto the beaches of California and other parts of the west coast, where Japan and other Far Eastern countries have also made huge investments and where real estate is still overvalued compared to the rest of the country. California is vulnerable to a large drop in real estate, although the shock will still be felt in other states and countries to a lesser degree.

When all the losses are toted up, we should find Japanese stocks have fallen down to the 4000 to 10,000 level on the Nikkei Dow, possibly even lower. Real estate in Japan should collapse anywhere from 50 to 80 percent from its peak values. Then we'll see real estate values drop from 30 to 70 percent in Hawaii, depending on the property. California real estate will plunge anywhere from 30 to 60 percent from its highs in 1989 and 1990. Since the Northeast has already been hard hit, and the markets of the South and Midwest never became overvalued, these sections of the country should suffer much lower drops in real estate.

A global recession

After that, the wave will continue rippling around the globe because Japanese investments in industry and real estate and businesses and government bonds have helped finance segments of the economy in every corner of the world. When Japan's money machine collapses, they won't have the high-value investment assets to cushion the shock. So they will have to retrench their investments and not make new ones. We'll see a huge deflationary recession worldwide.

Obviously this collapse will be a major event in Japan. The downturn in Japan will last for many years. They will suffer a turbulent shakeout in business—particularly in their banking system.

I've already told you that we've been in a recession because of the dip in baby boom spending. Now the tidal wave from Tokyo will exacerbate the worldwide deflation phenomenon and business shakeout, compounding the slowdown in baby boom buying. If we had a chance of coming out of our recession by late 1993, Tokyo's aftershocks will dampen that and increase the chances of a bottom in mid-to-late 1994.

In any case, as the world economy recovers in either 1993 or 1994, the Japanese will pull out of the recession much more slowly and with much more difficulty without the previous advantages of their money machine. This will be more like a prolonged depression in Japan.

The beginnings of the deflation we've seen in the United States in 1991 and 1992 and in other countries will reach new extremes in 1993, likely lasting into 1994 and beyond. Let's look at some of these effects worldwide.

The United States—a Chapter 11 economy Obviously, there will be utter devastation of real estate in California. Beyond that it's not a pretty picture either. Let's take a look.

A spike in interest rates. Capital contraction caused by the Japanese withdrawing their overseas investments will send interest rates up here into 1993—a few points on conservative government bonds and higher than that on corporate and higher-risk bonds. Because of this incredible capital squeeze I expect a 30-year Treasury bond that was as low as 7.2 percent in 1992 to go up toward 10 percent or higher. This will happen despite falling prices and the rapid decline of inflation, which normally precipitates falling interest rates—and will, after the crisis and recession are over.

Lack of consumer confidence. The deflation in real estate will hit homeowners and bite into their ability to purchase other durable goods. All consumers will become very cautious in spending and precipitate an even worse recession here at home. That will cause . . .

Falling prices. You can expect to see prices drop, not only in real estate but in oil, commodities, and goods and services from all businesses to some degree or other because of the huge shakeout and the cautiousness of consumers.

I expect the consumer price index to slide by 20 percent or more between 1993 and 1994, giving us the first sustained deflation we have seen since the '30s. We are likely to see strong deflation in 1993 and 1994, but we could continue to see prices trickling down into 1997 or 1998. This shock to the economy will have further reverberations.

Shakeout! Survival of the fittest. Falling prices always mean a heavy shakeout for businesses—weak businesses will quickly go under and be absorbed by the strong.

The chaos in business will lead to that Chapter 11 economy. Bankruptcies will be commonplace and not only in smaller businesses. From possibly even major banks to major industries, we'll watch the weaker firms failing. Banks trying to avoid writing off loans of failing companies will be looking for stronger firms to absorb those assets and some of the debt. Companies will change hands in consolidation moves. Our whole economy is going to go through that.

In every industry we will see the stronger, more liquid firms with good cost structures and established loyalty from their customers taking over the assets of the weaker firms. These more efficient, more profitable businesses will be perfectly positioned for the coming boom.

Rising unemployment. Any shakeout in business has its cost in lost jobs. We will see high unemployment, probably the highest since the Great Depression—12 to 14 percent between 1993 and 1994. Since the '80s and during the early stages of this recent recession, industrial firms have been cutting back. Agriculture is already lean and mean from past shakeouts. So recession won't hurt these industries as badly as in the past. Where, then, will most of these layoffs come from?

Two places. The greatest proportion of unemployment will hit services and government.

Service industries that did not shake out in the '80s and did not get hit as hard early on in the '90s recession—from law firms and accountants down to McDonald's and everybody else—will get blasted. Ditto for state and local governments and, ultimately, the federal government.

In a difficult recession, state and local governments, which don't have the financing and money-printing capacities of the federal government, will have to pare back programs and cut back staff. A shrinking military and demands for cuts in the federal bureaucracy will add to the unemployment rolls.

Cuts in federal programs. The federal government will be forced to cut expenditures. First of all, we'll hear more calls to accelerate defense cuts. Second, broader cuts into bureaucracy will inevitably mean reductions in services.

Consumers and businesses suffering from high interest rates are fed up with inefficiency. Citizens who see their companies and state and local governments making cutbacks will ask why the federal government can't get its house in order. I think there will be irresistible voter pressure for reductions.

A second pressure for federal cutbacks will come from international capital markets. As money gets scarce and the government deficit skyrockets, those capital markets are going to have increasing leverage with our government. If the federal government can show it is trying to cut costs, then capital markets will raise interest rates only 2 to 4 points. But if the government adopts highly inflationary, highly irresponsible borrowing policies and shows no willingness to cut back expenses to help lower its deficits, capital markets will raise interest rates 4 to 8 points.

When that happens, the government, forced to pay so much more for money, will be compelled to consider cuts.

A banking crisis. Deflation in real estate is obviously going to back up on the banks, particularly in California. Bankruptcies will cause banks to write off debt because they can't find buyers for failing companies.

That is bound to cause a shake-up in the banking industry. The federal government will have to intervene, leading to . . .

Soaring federal deficits. Now you can see why I earlier predicted deficits of $800 billion or higher by the federal government between 1993 and 1994. This will be one of the factors driving interest rates up in a very turbulent cycle when the federal government hogs the credit market during the downturn.

That's the recession in the United States. Now let's look elsewhere.

Europe   The economies of Europe, and particularly the struggling economies of the former Soviet Union and Eastern Europe, cannot afford a global recession. Europe has already seen slowing economic growth in 1992. The tidal wave from Tokyo will aggravate the difficulties of recovery for the former Communist countries. That's good news and bad news. The good news is that the added stress may force quicker, more effective changes in the economies by further weakening any old bureaucracies clinging to power. The bad news is that we could also see increased violence and attempts by the military or other factions to take over and restore not only order but some form of totalitarian rule.

So the European and Eastern European scenes are the least predictable during the tidal-wave scenario. Whatever the reaction of those countries, I see them as likely to come out of recession slowly at best in 1994 and more likely to remain in an ongoing restructuring process until the mid-1990s.

On top of that, you have the European Economic Community trying to achieve unity. This recession, I think, will in some ways, force them to do some things quicker. But in more ways, individual countries will pull back, becoming more protectionist and more skeptical in times of stress. Therefore, don't expect Europe to integrate with the lightning speed that many have predicted.

The greatest incentive for Europe to integrate will come when the United States emerges from the recession with such unexpected strength. That strong emergence will pose a powerful challenge to individual European countries and force them together just to compete credibly with the United States and North America.

The Middle East

I predict continued depressed conditions for the Middle East. The Arab countries are totally dependent on oil prices. When prices collapse, we'll see chaotic disruptions far into the future. We may have seen the end of the Cold War, but we haven't seen the end of hostilities in the Middle East.

Since Europe is on the edge of this difficult region, you have to expect European countries to have severe difficulties with the military skirmishes or outright warfare to the east and south.

In this worldwide recession, other Third World countries will also get hit somewhat by declining commodity prices. However, most of the Third World has been experiencing falling commodity prices since the '80s, so this recession will be more of the same for them.

The long-term global outlook is not a bust. Quite the contrary. Stay tuned for Chapter 7, "The Global Boom Scenario," where I'll discuss how the world will fare following the brief but brutal recession.

Weathering the recession in the United States

What can businesses and consumers do to prepare for the tidal wave from Tokyo? And how can they outlast the recession that's going to precede the greatest boom in history?

Unload stocks. If you still own stocks when this book comes out in January 1993, get rid of them. That will not be the time to be in the market. Liquidate stocks and bonds and any investments you can get out of.

Protect yourself in real estate. Anybody who can should protect their real estate investment with the best mortgage rates possible. If you refinance now use fixed rate mortgages and refinance again at lower rates around 1998. Try to get out of whatever real estate you can—though it may be too late. Be prepared for a significant recession. After all, if you're caught with drastic reductions in the value of your house or real estate, don't panic and sell at the bottom. Real estate prices will improve again as we move out of the recession by late 1994. If you buy at the bottom of the recession use variable rate mortgages.

Stop spending. Consumers, like any business, should cut back on expenditures, saving as much money as possible. This is a good time to reprioritize long-term family goals and to set up an effective budgeting system.

Lock in job security. Secure your job position. Start proving your value to your company so you'll be able to weather the tidal wave. There will be a lot of layoffs, white collar as well as blue collar. It's a time to make sure you're one of those people who aren't laid off.

Consolidate your business. If markets are still holding up, sell any assets you don't need in your business. Borrow any money now that you can from your bank before things get worse and credit dries up. Borrow money, not to use it, but to keep it as a recession hedge, a money chest. Cut your expenses, especially your overhead. But remain aggressive in marketing, sales, and R&D to gain market share at the expense of weaker competitors. Get as lean as possible so you can still try to generate profits or some cash flow during the aftermath of the tidal wave.

Invest wisely. The only really safe investment for your funds is personal or strategic assets you're going to keep long-term and short-term, interest-bearing government-backed securities like Treasury bills.

Bet on the boom

I think the most important thing you have to do is not believe those who will be spreading that inevitable depression gloom and doom. Economists and forecasters who were wrong in not anticipating this recession in the first place now will turn it into the great depression of all times. Some of them have already predicted the depression during the beginning stages of recession. The tidal wave from Tokyo will definitely reinforce the perception that there is something wrong with not only our country but the whole world economy. So it will give most people a gloomy outlook.

But . . .

If you're one of the consumers or businesses that have the best cash flow and decent balance sheets at the bottom of this recession between late 1993 and 1994, you are going to have incredible purchasing power opportunities. You're going to be able to buy real estate, stocks, bonds, assets of competitors, products—anything you want—at bargain basement prices at the bottom of this recession.

Smart consumers and businesses will be ready to invest at the bottom of this recession. If you have the guts, bet on the boom. Be willing to take risks. At times the most creative opportunities might present themselves to you. You may not even have to put out cash. You may encounter other consumers or other businesses or banks willing to give you assets in exchange for promises to pay over time. You may be able to acquire assets with no money down, just the perceived ability to pay for them at a time when other people can't.

The creative challenge will be to weather the tidal wave of recession, keeping your liquidity high and expenses low. Don't buy assets until you see the bottom of the trends I've predicted.

You'll read a lot more about how to invest wisely in Part II, "How to Profit in the Growth Boom of the '90s." The next two chapters, however, are critical to understanding how new technologies will eventually generate the growth economy into the 2000s.

5

The Innovation Wave

Predicting when new technologies will be adopted

BULLETIN

Each generation brings its own wave of innovations that move predictably into the economy. You can pin down the timetable for when such new products will take off. Imagine having a tool that could have foretold the moment to invest in radial tire stocks . . . or Xerox's photocopy process . . . or microcomputers . . . or the environmental movement . . . *or almost anything!*

Strap yourself in!

That's right, buckle up for a while because this chapter is central to understanding the rest of the book. Though not as sexy as the Spending Wave, the Innovation Wave is every bit as important. It establishes the context for what has come in the preceding chapters. And it builds a cumulative logic upon which every succeeding chapter rests. The Innovation Wave operates in conjunction with the Spending Wave and multiplies its power.

In this chapter we look at variations on a critical tool called the S-Curve, the basis for the Innovation Wave. As a business owner, once you know how S-Curves work you can predict where your own business will be going. As a manager, you can look into the future of the industries you have a stake in. As an investor, you can see where to put money in stock issues and in new growth markets of the '90s.

Again we begin by referring back to the fundamentals of . . .

The Generation Wave

We already saw how the Birth Wave is simply the charted births of a new generation. For baby boomers the wave features three surges or spikes in the birth rates. Chapter 2 addressed the Spending Wave, the most seductive of our forecasting tools. It tells us that a generation's spending patterns predict the direction of the economy and allows us to forecast the greatest boom in history.

Sandwiched between those two is the Innovation Wave. This wave peaks twenty-plus years after the peak of births of the generation—in other words, just as the generation is entering the work force. The S-Curve is the basic predictive tool of this wave. S-Curves show that a product's life cycle is not at all random. It follows a system, adhering to patterns repeated in hundreds of ways both small and large. Building on that idea, you will see how certain innovations cluster during the Innovation Wave of a generation's life cycle. You'll see how these clusters of innovations move with their companion generation's Spending Wave into the mainstream of the economy, following predictable paths and creating a cumulative effect.

Think about that last. Do you realize what predictable patterns for large clusters of important innovations can mean?

It means that when you know the correlation between innovations and generations, you can predict the rate at which new prod-

The Baby Boom Generation Wave

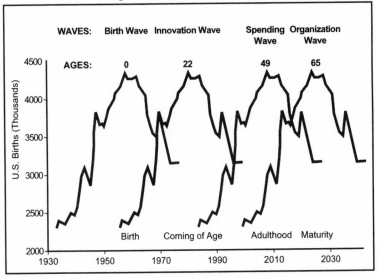

Figure 5-1. The Generation Wave revisited

ucts and innovations will grow, will be adopted, will mature. Imagine the ramifications of that insight! If you know the timetable of both individual and clustered products and technologies, you can take the guesswork out of those products' growth and development.

Reducing guesswork is critical because we're in the midst of an economic revolution more dramatic than the Industrial Revolution. That's right, even as we stand at the threshold of the greatest boom in history, we're already deeply into . . .

The Information Revolution

Some days you can sense a change for the better in your financial status. Other times you feel the economic ground slipping beneath your feet. As we've seen in the 1992 election year, with pollsters taking the pulse of America almost hourly, you're not alone in feeling uncertainty. Almost everybody feels moments of panic. That's because our present technological explosion seems so gradual and so random. And so contradictory. One day you'll read about trains designed to travel 200 miles an hour by "floating" on electromagnetic rails. The next day your flight will be delayed for an hour because of a stopped-up airplane toilet.

And what about the economy? You'd have to be blind not to see many of our older, mainstream industries going the way of the railroads. Heavy-manufacturing companies cut back on production and lay off staff. Large corporations hunker down, consolidating and reorganizing, processes that put people out of jobs. Companies fold—or buy one another at the cost of even more jobs. So in the midst of all these economic woes, you might well ask, "How can anybody say that we're on the threshold of a booming economy?"

I can understand how things might seem confusing to you. It's confusing to others too, including so-called experts. But believe me, many of the apparent contradictions in our economy can be explained with that S-Curve I referred to earlier.

When you understand S-Curves, the lights will come on. Suddenly you will realize that the turmoil of inflation in the '70s and '80s was meant to be. You will see that the deflation and the recession of the early 1990s were *supposed* to happen. You will recognize that our old economy must inevitably give way to a new one just as one generation of people gives way to the next.

S-Curves are so powerful I have begun using them as a context for analyzing many other processes of change, growth, and development. Let's look more closely at this fascinating tool.

The S-Curve

I didn't invent S-Curves, by the way. They've been used by technical, management, and academic people for quite a while. I simply put numbers on the S-Curve to make it easier for laypeople to see and understand the life cycles of products. Thus, it gives us the power to predict many aspects of the economy.

Here it is . . .

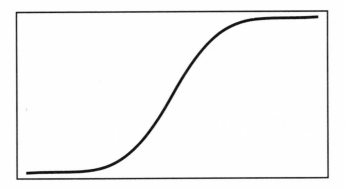

Figure 5-2. The S-Curve

Pretty simple and elegant, right? You'll be seeing a lot of this curve in this chapter. It's a fundamental tool for understanding the economy. Look at it again with some graphics and numbers added to help explain it further.

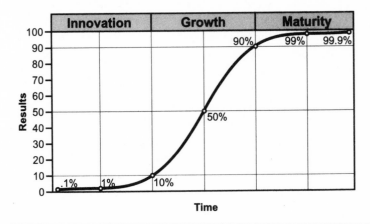

Figure 5-3. The S-Curve in detail

The vertical axis represents growth or results. The horizontal axis, divided into three equal stages, represents time. This leads to:

The Principle of the S-Curve

All new products and technologies go through three clear stages of growth: an Innovation phase, a Growth phase, and a Maturity phase. It takes the same time for a new technology or product to go from 0 to 10 percent (Innovation phase) of its potential market as it does from 10 to 90 percent (Growth phase) and as it does from 90 to 100 percent (Maturity phase).

This principle provides an enormous insight to businesses and investors. Clearly, the overwhelming majority of growth in any product's life cycle occurs in the concentrated period between 10 and 90 percent. The people who first spot this stage of vast opportunity are those who make most of the money because the Growth phase is where the fight for product or industry leadership is won or lost.

Examine the points I've marked along the S-Curve. Each of the major sections—Innovation, Growth, and Maturity—can be subdivided. Notice that the Growth section is divided both horizontally and vertically by the midpoint on the S-Curve. This means that it takes as long for a product to go from 10 to 50 percent as it does from 50 to 90 percent—the same distance in the same time. Later I'll show you that midpoint's significance as consumers adopt products into the mainstream economy.

Also look at the midpoints of the Innovation and Maturity phases. In the earliest part of the Innovation phase, it takes as long for a product to move from 0.1 percent adoption to 1 percent as it does later from 1 to 10 percent. Likewise, at the tail end of the Maturity phase, it takes as long for a product to move from 90 to 99 percent as it does to move from 99 to 99.9 percent. These are significant indicator points along the S-Curve.

Let's examine the major components of the S-Curve.

The Innovation phase   The lower end of the curve, the Innovation stage of a product or technology, is its invention and entrepreneurial phase. If you're an entrepreneur you already know that the very front end of product development consumes great gulps of resources—money, time, and energy. With very little to show for the investment.

Production of prototypes is experimental and costly. You suffer through design problems, obscurity, test marketing, manufacturing, and distribution. This is a very expensive process that leads to a costly product at first. So only a few sophisticated, affluent consumers who can afford it will want to adopt the product.

At this point, your new product or technology is usually regarded—if not dismissed—as a niche market, with less than 10 percent of market share.

The Growth phase   The steep section of the S-Curve from 10 to 90 percent is the sudden growth stage as your product or service is adopted rapidly into the mainstream economy. At this point some breakthrough innovation typically occurs, making the product far more affordable or accessible.

One factor that drives the S-Curve in this phase is consumer education. As people learn about the product or technology, it catches on. But a far more important factor driving growth is a drop in cost. Lower costs result from the increased consumer awareness, new economies of scale as production grows, and eventual competition with the resulting price wars.

After this growth, the product of technology enters maturity.

The Maturity phase   The top of the S-Curve shows how a product or technology levels off as the market becomes saturated. Certain die-hard consumers will never adopt it, so the S-Curve in practice never goes to 100 percent.

That's the basic theory laid out in generalities. Now let's look at a vivid example of how the S-Curve works in real life.

The bias against bias-ply tires

The first time I really saw the S-Curve in action I was consulting with Firestone as radial tires overtook bias-ply tires. In the early '70s, radial tires grew to 10 percent of the market in the United States. It took about seven years for this to happen, as you can see in Figure 5-4.

Firestone wasn't worried. The company knew radials were growing, but they never thought they would overtake their bias-ply tires and dominate the market. To Firestone, radials were merely a niche market. Who was buying them, after all? Not the masses, surely. Just a specialized group of drivers. A minority of consumers.

However, that minority of radials buyers just happened to be people who either drove European cars or were serious driving enthusiasts. They were performance-oriented drivers who owned high-performance cars. They spent more on performance tires than the average driver because they knew that radials were superior to bias-ply tires. Radials lasted longer, gave better traction, rode better, and were safer at high speeds.

Firestone, however, was betting that the reaction of the typical American consumer would be: "I ain't going to pay $300 for a set of tires when I can get a perfectly good set for $150."

In the next seven years, radials moved to 90 percent of the American tire market. Firestone kept building bias-ply plants— most of which they've since been forced to shut down. Now *there* was a company that didn't pay attention to what was happening. And Figure 5-4 shows what did happen to bias-ply tires.

Radials progressed slowly at first but really took off in the mid-'70s, so it doesn't look like the ideal S-Curve. In the 10 to 50 percent segment, growth was a bit slower to take off than on an ideal curve, owing to the 1973–1974 recession. However, the trend caught up with itself after the recession, experiencing a faster takeoff, moving sharply upward between 50 and 90 percent to hit its target right at the time the ideal curve would have predicted.

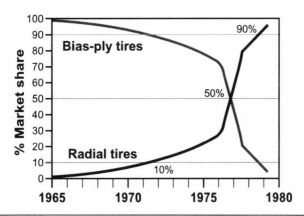

Figure 5-4. The radial tires S-Curve
Source: *Innovation,* Richard Foster

You get the picture. Rest assured, Firestone did. They are no longer a leader in their field because they missed the radial S-Curve. In fact, they were bought out by Bridgestone, a leading Japanese manufacturer of radials.

If Firestone had had the same access to the principle of the S-Curve as you now have, they could have seen they were wasting their investment in bias-ply tires. And you as an investor could have seen the rise of Michelin and Bridgestone as growth stocks. After six years, the wised-up American consumer had begun to figure out what the performance buyer had known for a long time. Once people caught on to the logic of a better value for their money, the emphasis switched to the safety of their families. You know the rest of the story, of course. You've been driving exclusively on radials for years, right?

This same set of dynamics applies to all the common products you're familiar with. Products like cars, televisions, dishwashers, fax machines, automatic teller machines, VCRs, compact disc players—all followed the S-Curve. Only the timetable varies from case to case.

Now let's take a closer look at one of the more famous, if not most influential, S-Curves in our economic history.

The classic S-Curve of
the automobile

I use the auto industry as an example because it is a fundamental technology that has helped define our economy since the turn of the century. It is also one of the better-documented S-Curves. Not to mention how well it conforms to the ideal.

Innovated in the late 1800s and early 1900s, automobiles grew into the mainstream, hitting their 10 to 90 percent growth phase from 1914 to 1928. Here in Figure 5-5 is the entire S-Curve from 1900 to 1942. Notice the seven-year increments marking the critical developments that brought cars down in cost so urban families could afford them. Keep in mind that automobiles affected the entire economy and other products of the period as well. So you could find many similarities between the S-Curve of autos and those of other products moving from niche markets into the mainstream at the time.

The Innovation phase of
the automobile

Before cars moved into commercial production in 1900, they were still merely an oddity, the toys of the wealthy and the eccentric, comprising only .1 percent of their eventual market.

Seven years later, in 1907, cars had grown to 1 percent of the urban population, just as the S-Curve would have predicted. Every seven years thereafter, the automobile moved up another predictable step on the S-Curve. People failed to foresee each successive growth stage. Not that they were stupid, mind you. It's just that we're trapped into the straight-line vision indicated by the Human Model of Forecasting. Because the innovations that were

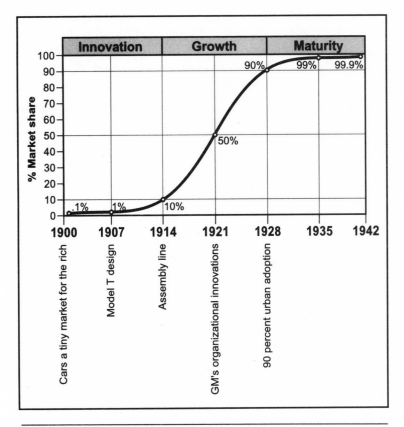

Figure 5-5. The classic automobile S-Curve
Source: *Recollecting the Future,* Hugh B. Stewart

to make these steps possible had not yet appeared, few people foresaw the growth to come.

The first key innovation, in 1907, was Henry Ford's standardized Model T design, which brought down the cost of owning a car. By 1914, 10 percent of urban families were able to afford cars.

In that same year, the breakthrough innovation occurred. This innovation wasn't a product, though. It was a process, an organizational innovation—the moving assembly line. Henry Ford realized he could build standardized, high-quality products on an assembly line—and much more efficiently than before. With that realization, Ford brought the manufacturing cost down and opened the doors for the automobile to become a mass-market item. The day he successfully introduced the assembly line to the manufacture of automobiles, Henry Ford cut the price of a Model T in half while doubling the wages of his workers. Continued cost reductions allowed 50 percent of urban families to own cars by 1921.

The rise of General Motors

From 1921 on, General Motors led the innovation process with the organizational design innovations of Alfred Sloan. The Model T was the primary car available from Ford. But GM introduced variety to its car lines. For the first time, people could choose from a number of styles and options and trade up to higher-quality cars as their incomes rose with the aging of that generation. And GM kept engineering incremental improvements in all aspects of its cars.

Perhaps the most notable innovation of all was installment financing of cars. After that, virtually everyone could afford an automobile. By 1928, 90 percent of urban families had cars—and GM won the race for emerging leadership in the auto industry. Not only that, installment financing and hundreds of automobile-related industries began to sweep the country, making this the century of the car. Not to mention the century of installment debt.

As people learn more about the power and applications of the S-Curve, they will know both when the next innovation is about to occur and when the takeoff period of growth will happen.

Let's go a couple of steps further so you can understand the S-Curve well enough to apply its potential in forecasting the progress of new products and technologies. Who knows? Perhaps you have at your fingertips another innovation with the potential of radial tires. If so, these principles should help you recognize your position.

Let's start by looking at what drives the S-Curve.

Two forces driving the S-Curve

1. Consumer adoption patterns   It's as much a human tendency for consumers to resist new products as it is to resist new ideas, I suppose. Any marketer will tell you it takes education and familiarity over a period of time to get consumers to buy. What any marketer may not tell you is that this consumer adoption pattern follows the S-Curve. That means we can predict when a product will take off.

There's no rocket science or economic mumbo jumbo here in the following graph, another refinement of the basic S-Curve.

You see by the arrow on the graph that new technologies move

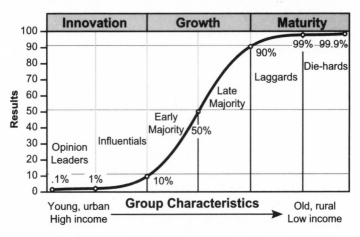

Figure 5-6. Consumer adoption patterns

from young to old, urban to rural, and from higher-income groups to lower-income groups, as a rule. Think about it. In general, who are the first to adopt new products? For example, take VCRs. Usually younger people, and especially younger people with money, adopt them first, right? These early adopters usually come from urban or affluent suburban areas. Why? Because cities are where the numbers and the trendsetters are. The greater the concentration of a population, the greater the likelihood of finding more sophisticated consumers and specialty stores that can cater to them. Now a brief word about each of the categories on the graph.

Opinion Leaders—1 percent   These people are professionals or hobbyists in new technologies, new products, and social trends. Who bought the first VCRs? Electronics buffs, of course. Movie freaks. Television junkies. Television industry analysts, critics, and employees . . . a small minority of technologically sophisticated insiders who knew the potential and excitement of such machines. Remember, industrial-strength video recorder-players had already existed for a long time in television studios in one-inch and three-quarter-inch formats. When VCRs became consumer items, only a few people had seen them used in the editing, replaying, and storing of video images. These became the Opinion Leaders in consumer adoption. Opinion Leaders start trends by being the first to adopt new products and technologies.

Influentials—1 to 10 percent   These people tend to immerse themselves in their world, keeping in touch with new trends. Influentials know what's hot.

Influentials are the people who must own every kind of gadget imaginable—and *now!* They adopt experimental products, hang the cost. Then they launch their word-of-mouth networks. With the adoption of the VCR, you saw trade journals and high-tech magazines, then general journalism picking up the story. Eventually new products saturate their niche markets—sometimes called yuppie markets. That's the sign they are approaching the takeoff stage near the 10 percent point of market penetration. When the upper-middle-class markets start to show interest, watch out!

Early Majority—10 to 50 percent   These upper-middle-class people, usually from the suburbs, have the discretionary bucks to spend on a product. They'll try to be the first on their block to own one. Mind you, they don't take the risk of buying until the product has proven its benefits and reliability in niche markets. And, of course, they wait for the price to drop somewhat. In effect, they watch what the influentials are doing and follow. Their adoption of the product kicks off major growth in the S-Curve.

Late Majority—50 to 90 percent   These folks pooh-poohed the VCR in the beginning. Or they didn't have the discretionary income to blow on creating their own television reruns. Or the early technology seemed to be too confusing to them. The Late Majority is the true mass market, for obvious reasons. Once they follow the Early Majority in adopting products, they push the percentages up over 50 percent toward 90 percent. Products that arrive at this stage will be widely available in stores like Sears, Wal-Mart, and Kmart.

Laggards—90 to 99 percent   Laggards won't own the new product until their children buy it as a gift for them, or until their favorite older products are no longer available or cost more than the new product. These are usually not going to be sophisticated adopters. You've heard the stories about the grandparents getting a VCR they now use as a digital clock (that sometimes stays blinking on 12:00 P.M.).

Die-hards   These folks in the hills and hollows of the American outback may never adopt new technologies. It's a matter of principle, not cost.

So much for the consumer adoption pattern applied to the S-Curve. Let's look at a second factor driving the S-Curve—cost.

2. The blessings of the Cost Curve   Falling costs drive the S-Curve too. When you think about it, what else? Lower prices are a universal force in consumer adoption. Everybody who's ever

bought into new technology understands cost. When new products and technologies appear, they are expensive. The first VCRs cost two and three times as much as the top-of-the line machines nowadays. The same is true of most products. And cost shifts are just as predictable as the S-Curve progression.

Experts in cost dynamics use a proven principle that can be stated as a simple rule of thumb:

> Every time the cumulative number of units produced doubles, its cost drops 20 to 30 percent. After the bugs have been ironed out of the early models, and the competitive fires are lit, new technologies increasingly can be had at bargain basement prices.

It should be obvious that as the cost of a product comes down, broader segments of the population will be attracted to it. In fact, when the Cost Curve crosses the S-Curve, the Late Majority adopts the product, making it a true mass-market item.

You now have the fundamentals of individual S-Curves and Cost Curves. It is time to discuss the interaction of curves.

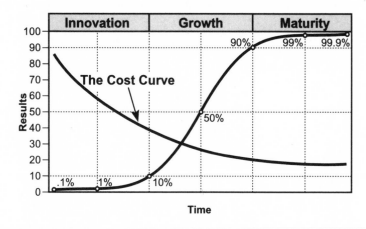

Figure 5-7. The Cost Curve

When new S-Curves appear

As a general rule, new S-Curves will emerge in the maturity stage of an old S-Curve's cycle. This is portrayed in Figure 5-8.

> When an old technology is maturing, in its 90 to 100 percent phase of adoption, you usually see a newer version of that technology emerging in its 0 to 10 percent innovation stage. Those stages overlap only temporarily. After the new breaks into its 10 to 90 percent phase, it then rapidly overtakes the old.

Refer back to the example of radials overtaking bias-ply tires. I've redrawn Figure 5-4 to show exactly the same relationship, but this time using two S-Curves that overlap like those in Figure 5-8.

We see this kind of overlap in all types of technologies, products, and services throughout history—ranging from automobiles overtaking railroads in the past to CDs replacing records in the present.

Bias and Radial S-Curves

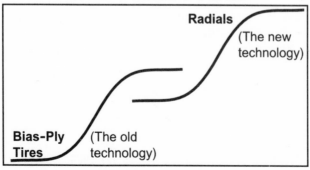

Figure 5-8. Overlapping S-Curves of bias-ply and radial tires

If we look at the entire history of computers in Figure 5-9, it's clear we can identify an S-Curve for mainframe computers originating in the '50s and maturing in the mid-'70s and '80s. In the mid-'70s and '80s we also saw the emergence of the next S-Curve, microcomputers.

I think it's obvious to most of us that microcomputers will dominate the growth of the computer industry in the coming decades. But remember, it wasn't so obvious to most mainframe computer companies until well into the '80s. And I've got a flash for you . . .

> The main explosion in the microcomputer revolution has yet to happen! We will see a second S-Curve of microcomputers, as portable, or notebook, machines grow in power and numbers—until the inevitable superpowered hand-held computer arrives to eventually diminish every other once-startling aspect of the computer revolution into insignificance.

S-Curves for Mainframes and Microcomputers

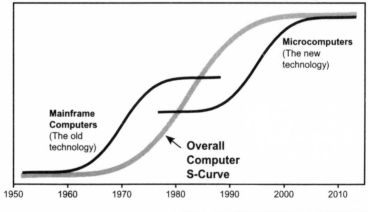

Figure 5-9. Overlapping S-Curves of mainframes and microcomputers

So let's look closer at the microcomputer S-Curve in Figure 5-10, which is the key technology driving the Innovation Wave of baby boomers. The baby boom generation's Spending Wave, beginning in the 1980s and lasting into the 2000s, will see two overlapping S-Curve phases within the overall S-Curve of the microcomputer.

The first wave of microcomputer innovations was the desktop version commonly known as the personal computer. Its innovation phase came in the mid-'70s and early '80s. Its growth, or 10 to 90 percent, phase was in the early-to-late '80s. In the late '80s and early '90s we have seen the growth of personal computers slowing. What did that computer do? Desktops primarily automated the office, an advance considered nearly complete, even in many smaller businesses.

Meanwhile you can already see an emerging second phase of the microcomputer revolution—portable computers: laptop, notebook, and palmtop. These new models won't be confined to a niche line of microcomputers. Indeed, they will dominate computer sales in the next decade.

Why? Because the laptop and notebook computers will now be able to leave the office. Look for sales, customer service staff, and mobile professionals—the real front-line areas of business that have the greatest impact on customers—to take the company to the customer with these computers.

This trend will allow reductions in bureaucracies and indirect jobs to degrees simply unforeseen today. White-collar work will be automated in the coming decades just as blue-collar and farm work were automated in the past—not by making those jobs more efficient, but by eliminating them through programming those functions into the software used in portable computers on the front lines.

Look for the takeoff stage of laptop and notebook computers and field automation software between 1995 and 1997, shortly after the end of the recession. In computers, an industry undergoing a considerable shakeout and confusion, we should be able to see that the notebook computer and the related areas of sales and field

S-Curves for Desktop and Portable PCs

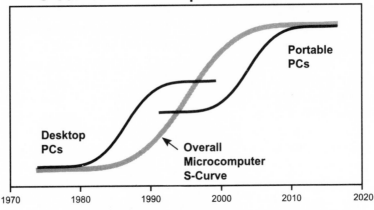

Figure 5-10. Overlapping S-Curves within microcomputer evolution

automation software are where to invest. That's where the growth is going to come in the next decade. We should expect the 10 to 90 percent phase of these computers to come from the mid-90s into the early 2000s. We'll be seeing business conducted under an entirely new set of assumptions, an area I'll address in Chapter 11.

Now, just for the sake of illustration, let's put the entire computer S-Curve picture together in Figure 5-11.

This figure summarizes the overlapping S-Curves within the entire computer spectrum. You can see the evolution of computer products to date, an evolution you're probably familiar with intuitively. That's how S-Curves overlap and interact.

Cost Curves overlap too. And the second Cost Curve adds new dimensions to our developing picture.

S-Curves for All Computers

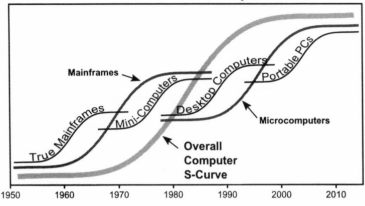

Figure 5-11. Overall product evolution of computers summarized

Overlapping cost dynamics

Now that you understand how new S-Curves overlap old ones, you can better understand the cost dynamics that drive new products to rapidly overtake old ones. Figure 5-12 shows how predictable Cost Curves overlap just as S-Curve growth patterns overlap.

As I've said before, a breakthrough innovation of a product or technology will come in at higher costs, and therefore at premium prices. In its early stages, the breakthrough will quickly be coming down its Cost Curve while the old makes very slow progress. At some point, the new product becomes competitive in price and ultimately less expensive than the older product in most markets. As the premium starts shrinking, the Early Majority starts to buy— that correlates to the launching of the 10 to 50 percent growth phase. When the new product becomes cheaper than the old product, the Late Majority starts buying. That forces the product to move through its 50 to 90 percent growth phase.

In steel production, mini-mills are a perfect example of this Cost

The Dual-Cost Curve Leading to Lower Prices

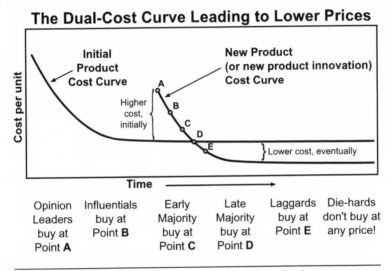

Figure 5-12. Overlapping Cost Curves and the adoption process

Curve phenomenon. In the early '80s I was consulting to a large steel company. At that time mini-mills could only compete in regional construction markets because they turned out low-value products, saving money in transportation costs and using cheaper scrap steel inputs. The larger steel companies never considered mini-mills to be a serious competitor for their mainstream automotive and can markets—precisely because the costs of production were too high. But with experience and economies of scale, such mini-mills have greatly lowered their costs while improving their quality. Now they approach point D in Figure 5-12, competing with large mills in mainstream markets. It is just a matter of time before they dominate most steel markets. This will return the competitive edge in steel back to the United States through companies like Nucor and Chapparal, which dominate mini-mill steel production. See what I mean about centralized planning in Japan leading to low-profit investments in industries that will be dead ends in the long run!

The biggest mistake any company or investor can make is to assume that a premium-priced or niche product of today will not come down in price and move into the mainstream markets in the future. Only by tracking a product's progress on its S-Curve can you effectively forecast the growth of critical new products and technologies into the mainstream. If you're watching the commonly studied symptoms that most businesses and investors track, you will only be convinced that these markets have little potential. You won't see such a growth market until after the breakthrough innovation, which is often too late.

Here's yet another concept to enlarge on S-Curves.

Tying generations to new clusters of technologies

Every 40 to 50 years, clusters of innovations appear as new generations come of age. These clusters occur partly because the younger generation, with a fresh spirit of entrepreneurship, invents new things. Also, younger people challenge old ideas and generate new ones as they move into the school systems. Innovation is basically generated by the natural friction between the idealistic ideas of the new generation and the realistic feedback, criticism, and outright rejection of the old generation. Out of this process, new ideas move into the R&D labs and begin to take shape as tangible products and technologies. The first manifestations are generally broad-scale breakthroughs in fundamental areas like transportation, communications, and energy that scientists call basic innovations. Such basic innovations pave the way for many practical inventions that follow. Examples of basic innovations include the steam engine, electrical energy, railroads, television, the

internal-combustion engine, the telephone, the transistor that led
to consumer electronics and mainframe computers, and the semiconductor chip that led to microcomputers.

Figure 5-13 shows how innovations occur in distinct clusters. It
also shows that the last three clusters in innovations coincided with
the three generations prior to the baby boom.

The Bob Hope generation, which grew up in the Great Depression and fought World War II as they were coming of age, invented the television, the jet engine, the mainframe computer,
consumer electronics, automatic home appliances like washers
and dryers, the A-bomb, radar, and—for the automobile—
power brakes, power steering, automatic transmissions, and
superhighways in the '30s and '40s. These became the major
growth industries of the '50s and '60s during that generation's
spending boom.

The Henry Ford generation in the late 1800s and early 1900s
gave us the automobile, the telephone, electrical energy, canned

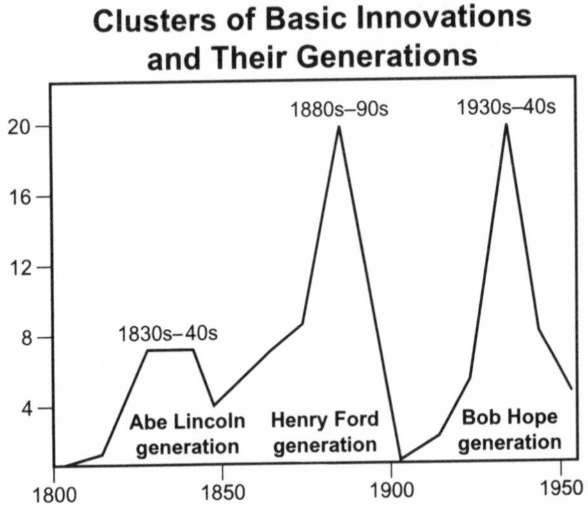

Clusters of Basic Innovations and Their Generations

Figure 5-13. Clusters of basic innovations for
three past generations
Source: Gerhard Mensch

foods, movies, radio, the phonograph, and propeller-driven air-planes—to name a few. In that generation's spending boom between 1900 and the Roaring Twenties, these grew into major industries. The innovations of this generation had the broad-based effect of decentralizing society, or, ultimately, allowing us to move to the suburbs.

The Abraham Lincoln generation before that brought us rail-roads, the telegraph, and basic steel production, which were the major growth industries just prior to and following the Civil War.

In every case, such a cluster of basic innovations is followed by an entrepreneurial period. Innovators tackle the creative challenge of putting basic technologies to work in business and industry. They try to make money with the new ideas and discoveries.

To summarize, with every generation comes new clusters of technologies, products, and services that become the growth industries during that generation's spending boom. That's a unique aspect of boom periods like the coming one, so let me restate it.

When a generation causes a boom, it is a boom in the products they innovated, not in mature products that have been consolidating in older industries. Most people assume that in any boom the good old industries of the past from Sears to Corn Flakes to IBM mainframes are just going to grow with that boom. That is not the case now, any more than it was for the railroads in the 1920s or for propeller planes in the commercial airline industry of the '50s and '60s. New inno-vations move into niche markets, or the 0 to 10 percent phase of the S-Curve, during the new generation's Innovation Wave. They move into the mainstream markets, or the 10 to 90 percent phase of the S-Curve, during the generation's Spending Wave.

During the boom period of a new generation, new growth prod-ucts even more rapidly overtake older industries. In this coming boom, mature industries will see the ground beneath them shift even more suddenly. Emerging products and technologies will grow so fast that many of the old will be relegated to niche markets by the end of this boom. Some will decline into oblivion.

Let's see how all the factors we've discussed so far are related.

S-Curves, generations, and clusters of technology

Figure 5-14 shows the S-Curves of today's two relevant generations—the Bob Hope generation and the baby boom generation—and how they overlap.

As the Bob Hope generation's spending boom topped out in the late '60s, most of the industries associated with that generation—first automobiles and later mainframe computers—entered their maturity phase. Right in time with this slowdown in the S-Curve, the economy turned down into a long-term recessionary period into the early 80s. Put in S-Curve terms, the innovations of the

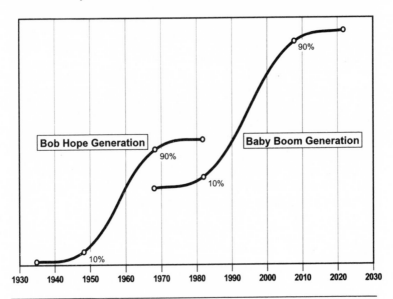

Figure 5-14. Two generations overlap

Bob Hope generation had entered their 90 to 100 percent phase.

Meanwhile the baby boom generation's Innovation Wave was in its 0 to 10 percent phase, a time of high investment and low productivity. This created economic stagnation. In the '70s and early '80s we saw breakthrough innovations like the microcomputer. Also an entrepreneurial revolution has established new growth markets in virtually every industry. These clusters of new products and technologies will continue to cruise through their 10 to 90 percent growth phase with the baby boomers' Spending Wave, intensifying in 1994 and lasting until 2006 to 2010.

If we lay the Spending Waves of both generations over their S-Curves, we get Figure 5-15, which shows how both generations' new products and innovations are adopted in sync with each generation's spending pattern.

Here's the critical point: The Spending Wave cycle of each generation, combined with its cluster of new products and technologies moving into the 10 to 90 percent segment of their markets, creates

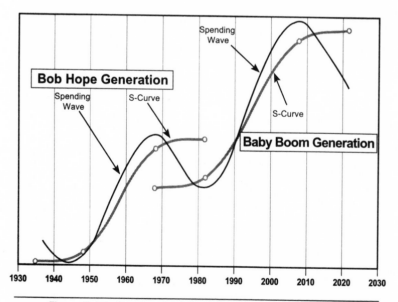

Figure 5-15. Synchronized Spending Waves and S-Curves
forming the Innovation Wave

a powerful boom period. This is the bottom line to the Spending Wave I discussed in Chapter 2 when I said it would lead to the greatest boom in history. Just think of the power of the huge baby boom generation's Spending Wave when it is combined with the most powerful innovations in history moving through their fastest growth phase!

The atomic structure of business

If we summarize all aspects of the S-Curves and the Innovation Wave, we can see there is a four-stage progression. In its simplest application, I call this tool the product life cycle. It is the basic building block of business.

These four phases of alternating progress or profits are related to booms and busts as shown in Figure 5-16.

The innovation phase. This is the radical innovation or birth phase of a new product or technology. It is typically a period of low profit or, more likely, negative cash flow as the product or technology gets off the ground. During this phase, a new product struggles to become viable in a functional design at a

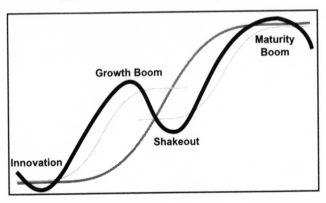

Figure 5-16. The product life cycle that evolves from the Innovation Wave

low enough cost to sell. Then it seeks the niche markets that will accept it.

Growth boom. This is a time when the new product makes its first move out of niche markets into the mainstream. Typically this period is dominated by the purchasing power of Early Majority buyers. It is generally a time of high margins and high growth that attracts competitive entry of a lot of businesses, accounting for the steepest growth and greatest profitability in the S-Curve. This boom can be described as a barroom brawl, with rapid growth, continual incremental innovation, furious competition, and fat margins—much more dynamic than the maturity boom that comes later.

But as growth progresses, economies of scale and brand awareness advantages grow, so smaller and less efficient firms find it increasingly difficult to compete.

Shakeout. After growth boom spending peaks out, the shakeout of competitors accelerates dramatically. At the top of the growth boom, most businesses add capacity. Think of this as an arms buildup in the war for market share and eventual dominance. When spending by the Early Majority slows, the excess capacity thus created results in a cataclysmic price war. The weaker firms go belly-up rapidly. This is the mid-life crisis in a technology.

This shakeout usually creates a period of uncertainty. Even so, it has a positive outcome, shifting market share to the stronger firms so they can take advantage of even greater cost efficiencies in preparation for the next boom period. It's the economic equivalent of Darwin's survival of the fittest. Shakeouts are marked by price wars, high rates of business failures, cutbacks in company spending, and layoffs in staff.

Meanwhile, a second period of innovation has been occurring within the shakeout. In Figure 5-16, the small S-Curve in the lower left represents the original—or radical—innovation. The small S-Curve in the upper right represents the second round of incremental innovations within the overall S-Curve of the product development that improve upon the original design and extend the product into broader and even more affordable applications.

Maturity boom. When spending resumes, the larger surviving competitors bring the prices of products down so far that they move into mass markets until full saturation. This phase of the cycle is more like a ballroom dance in comparison with the barroom brawl of the growth boom. Only a few gentlemanly firms tend to dominate each mass market. For example, in the auto industry, there were as many as two hundred car companies coming out of the innovation phase and into the growth boom. After the shakeout and in the maturity boom, that number shook down to only a handful by the end of World War II.

Then the cycle repeats itself. New, radical innovations move into niches as the older, maturing products begin their decline.

Extending the power of the product life cycle

Figure 5-17 shows how the product life cycle works when applied to clusters of baby boom technologies for the coming decades. The innovation phase preceded the boom in the '70s and early '80s. The growth boom phase occurred from 1982 to 1990. That's history, of course. But any analysis of the shakeout we've been experiencing is more than looking at history. As we watch the shakeout conform to the behavior of past economic trends in this life cycle, we're given a glimpse into the future. There's more to this than the gloom and doom you've been hearing about. There's actually good news in this current shakeout, which began in 1990 and which will extend no later than 1994. The end is in sight! Our new forecasting tool reliably predicts that in 1993 or 1994 we'll see a reversal of trends. Even better, the end of chaos will launch the current cluster of products and technologies into their maturity boom within the baby boom Spending Wave lasting until 2006 to 2010, as Figure 5-17 shows.

This figure is the culmination of logic that began with the simple

Baby Boomer Product Life Cycle

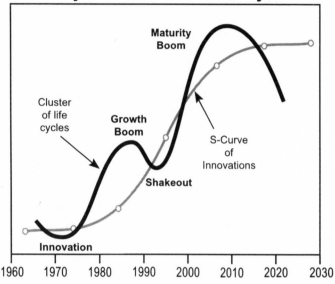

Figure 5-17. Product life cycle showing how clusters of baby boom technologies will develop to maturity during the greatest boom in history

S-Curve of Chapter 2. It has become your window to the future! Here's what this startling little figure means to you:

You now have the power to identify innovations in emerging markets. You can pinpoint those that will generate rapid growth in their industries as we come out of the recession and enter the second phase of the greatest boom in history. In industries you are familiar with, you already know which products and technologies have already arrived at about 10 percent of market share in their innovation stages. You simply calculate the length of time it took to move from 0 to 10 percent and extend it forward to see how long the boom—in its 10 to 90 percent phase—will last. Likewise, you can easily predict the shakeout, which normally occurs between the 30 percent and 50 percent point of market penetration. You can consolidate beforehand, avoiding shell shock when original products mature. During this consolidation period, you simply keep your eyes peeled for the incremental innovations that will carry surviving companies and refurbished products and technologies into the maturity boom. Armed with your industry expertise and the road map of the product life cycle, you should be able to use this powerful tool to actually look into the future!

As a rule, the typical emerging product or service today is in its shakeout phase, getting ready to move into the maturity boom that will last from 1994 out to 2006 to 2010. We'll give more examples in Chapter 9. Depending on the product, the precise timing will differ, of course. But we're talking about the main cluster of innovations.

In the next chapter, I will expand the S-Curve concept even further to show how broader industry cycles form and change our overall economy in predictable ways.

6

The New Customized Economy

*Sweeping changes return
the economic advantage
to America*

BULLETIN

The economy as we know it is about to be
revolutionized! Our present Standardized Economy will
give way to a new Customized Economy. This new
economy will accentuate the skills of U.S. businesses
and baby boomers and return America to preeminence
in the world economy.

The story of the economy is the
story of human behavior

Let's return to the bottom line here. *People count!*

This book is about nothing if it is not about people—and how
the predictable path of human behavior drives our economy. Yes,

I've introduced concepts like the Spending Wave, the Innovation Wave, and S-Curves. But those concepts don't conform to the laws of physics like the planets in our solar system or the stars in the heavens. No, these waves and curves are simple shorthand expressions of predictable human behavior. That is, we can predict when people will spend. We can see patterns in how they will adopt products, if we use the proper tools. Waves and curves are merely my system for analyzing, organizing, and discussing those behaviors—but you already understand them intuitively.

After all, each of us plays a part in the processes I'm talking about. For example, before I ever mentioned my observations about consumer adoption patterns, you already knew where you were in buying a VCR. But my stories aren't about VCRs or cars or computers—they're about people. This material isn't just about metal and plastic and silicone chips. Waves and curves don't cause booms and busts. People do. We should keep that in mind as we tackle the macro-topics of generations, industry cycles, and economies.

Alternate generation cycles start new economies

Let's start with the big picture. My conclusion is that our economy has been on the move, shifting like one of the tectonic plates in the earth's crust. The Innovation Wave of every other generation brings us clusters of radical new technologies. These clusters form new industries that build the foundations and set directions for a new economy. So economies are simply clusters of industries related and united by sets of fundamental new technologies, and management and production processes that follow the simple four-stage product life cycle. The automobile is a perfect example of how certain innovations cluster at a given time in a generation's life cycle. The car spawned entire industries built around components like tires and services like repairs and tune-ups. Related industries included the construction of superhighways. And, of course, the oil industry burgeoned to provide petroleum products.

Whereas I said before that every individual product has its own timetable, the economy is on a longer timetable. Two generations, to be precise. Here's how it works.

Two generations ago, Henry Ford's generation ushered in the economy that was extended to its present maturity by the Bob Hope generation. Baby boomers are introducing a new economy that will be extended by the following generation.

What will this new economy look like? It will assume the personality of baby boomers at the outset. Eventually baby boomers will give way to the "Millennial" generation born in the '80s and '90s. Millennials, a term introduced by William Strauss and Neil Howe in *Generations,* will extend this economy into its maturity with their Innovation and Spending waves.

We can better understand why this happens by simply looking at the historic generation cycle documented by Strauss and Howe in Figure 6-1.

Throughout our history we've seen this alternating generation cycle. You will always see an inner-directed, individualistic, entrepreneurial generation followed by an outer-directed, conformist, more civic-minded generation. For example, the Henry Ford gen-

The Alternating Cycle of Generations

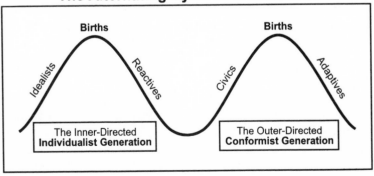

Figure 6-1. The two-generation cycle
Source: *Generations,* William Strauss and Neil Howe

eration born from the 1860s to the early 1880s was such an inner-directed generation. I call them Individualists. The Bob Hope generation born from the late 1890s to the early 1920s was an outer-directed generation. I call them Conformists. The baby boom generation is the current example of an inner-directed generation. So the Millennial generation will be the next Conformist generation. Now I want to show you how these generations and the technologies of their times are interrelated. To me, the following is a striking insight.

Generations are engines of change. It's obvious to us all that each generation has its own technologies, lifestyles, personalities, and behaviors that form a distinctive social character. When you examine an economy in the context of characteristics of a generation, the evidence continues to mount for human behavior driving the economy!

Now let's examine these relationships between generations and technologies to see how economies are formed.

Each new economy follows the same four-stage cycle of innovation; growth boom; shakeout; and maturity boom that we discussed for a product life cycle in Chapter 5. The Individualist generation's Innovation Wave coincides with and actually causes the innovation phase of the economy. Its Spending Wave causes the growth boom phase of the economy. So the Innovation Wave and Spending Wave of the Conformist generation will also form the shakeout and maturity boom phases, respectively.

The inner-directed Individualist generation
The two-generation cycle begins with Individualists. The members born in the rising tide of births of this generation, called Idealists, tend to be more radical as innovators. They concentrate on social changes. They set entirely new directions for society. As they grow up, Idealists tend to attack the old, mature values, infrastructures, and institutions of the past. These are also leaders who dare to move

into uncharted waters. The declining tide of this Individualist generation, called Reactives, are equally, if not more, individualistic but react to the idealistic nature of the rising tide and are, therefore, more pragmatic and management-oriented. So the Idealists build new growth companies, and the Reactives manage and consolidate them.

Individualists perform better as self-motivators and entrepreneurs who start up new enterprises. The Henry Ford generation, for example, came up with the most radical new technology of their times, the automobile. Henry Ford himself was probably the greatest innovator of his generation. Although he didn't invent the automobile, he brought the concept of the moving assembly line to the industry, ushering automobiles into mainstream affordability. The assembly line, in turn, became the basis for the growth boom phase of the automobile and most other emerging industries in the 1920s. That was then the biggest leap in business innovation. In effect, Henry Ford redefined transportation and business.

The outer-directed Conformist generation The generation that follows the Individualist is just the opposite in character to it. The outer-directed Conformist generation always reacts to the individualism of the inner-directed generation. They resist individualism and a fragmented society. They seek unity.

The rising tide of this generation, called Civics, are can-do, society-oriented institution builders. This group's innovations improve upon the entrepreneurial innovations and growth organizations developed by the previous generation, moving them into the mainstream. Their innovations are incremental. They broaden and extend the growth industries built by Individualists rather than create a radical new direction.

Individualists put innovations on the map. Conformists take innovations into mass markets, making them affordable so everybody can own the product, and often more than one. Civics built our Fortune 500 companies, which in the times of the Henry Ford generation were either growth businesses or entrepreneurial companies, not mainstream, mass-market institutions. Between the two generations, the economy undergoes a period of turbulence I call a shakeout. The time between Henry Ford's generation and Bob Hope's was the Great Depression.

As the economy matures—eventually stagnating—Adaptives, those born in the declining tide of the Conformist generation, administer the institutions of society built by the Civics, the rising phase of that generation. The Adaptives of the Bob Hope generation have been running our corporations for the last ten to twenty years.

That's a complete cycle. Industries built along these cycles can be charted using our familiar S-Curves. The next set of generations in the cycle equivalent to the Henry Ford and Bob Hope generations will be the Individualist baby boom generation and the follow-on incremental innovators, the Conformist Millennial generation.

Standardized versus Customized

We're moving toward a new economy. The present economy was shaped by the Henry Ford and Bob Hope generations. I call it the Standardized Economy. I call the new economy the Customized Economy. This is a good place to distinguish between the two.

Economies are merely clusters of related industries that operate with similar technologies and management formulas and move together through the same four-stage cycle of innovation, growth, shakeout, and maturity.

> The macrocycle of innovation, growth, shakeout, and maturity explains why we have alternating periods of inflation and deflation. Inflation accompanies and finances the innovation phase, and depression or deflation accompanies the shakeout phase.

We just talked about the automobile. It was only one of many innovations in the cluster of innovations that formed the Standardized Economy. This cluster of innovations of the Henry Ford generation—from cars to many of our present brand names—was perpetuated by the Bob Hope generation. Here's a summary definition of . . .

THE STANDARDIZED ECONOMY

The Standardized Economy consists of countless varieties of products, but they all result from a common economic formula. That formula is one of mass-produced, standardized goods and services made cheaper by assembly-line production.

This production was supervised by functional management organizations, management by assembly line—a different group performing individual functions like R&D, marketing, sales, and so on. Such organizations grew into larger and larger corporations making progressively bigger investments in heavy machinery. Productivity was driven by those enormous hardware investments in large machinery that ran faster and faster and burned more and more natural resources like oil and coal to provide energy.

The result of such an economy has been the longer, faster production runs putting out standard-quality goods at cheaper prices, making them affordable to greater numbers of consumers.

That economy launched America into world industrial leadership. But it predictably matured with the end of the spending boom of the Bob Hope generation and the saturation of our consumers and mass markets with standardized goods and services.

This is the economy we have been living in till now.

The coming Customized Economy

In the '70s and '80s, as the Japanese were perfecting the Standardized Economy in its maturing phase, the next entrepreneurial generation, baby boomers, moved into its Innovation Wave and brought radical new innovations, principally the microcomputer. That has established the foundation of the next economy, which I call the Customized Economy. A whole range of customized, high-quality products will be accelerating into our economy with the Spending Wave of the baby boom generation in the next two decades.

Because baby boomers will be shaping a new economy that will dominate for many decades, the personality of the economy will reflect that of this Individualist generation.

THE INEVITABLE NEW CUSTOMIZED ECONOMY

We've been creating an entirely new economy on top of the old. The microcomputer industry and a broad range of new niche products and services will increasingly dominate our economy in the coming decades. Microtechnologies increasingly allow us to custom-design, market, and produce products and services at lower cost.

The new economy, shown in Figure 6-2, will be characterized by companies that organize around the front lines of their organizations. It's at the front line where more products and services will be designed, produced, and delivered—the precise opposite principle of the Standardized Economy. Productivity will be driven by investments in flexible software and will use information as the fuel. The result: we will see customized products and services become more affordable than our standardized products and services of today.

This new economy will launch America into world leadership after the Japanese have bested us in the past decades of the maturing phase of the Standardized Economy. This Customized Economy will not mature until the peak of the Millennial generation's Spending Wave, sometime in the late 2040s. This Millennial generation will most likely innovate methods for truly mass-producing

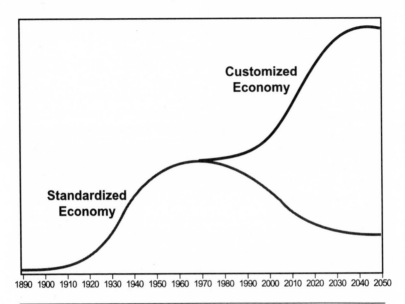

Figure 6-2. The Customized Economy that has been forming
over the declining Standardized Economy

customized products and services, thereby moving them into mass
markets.

We can see this pattern of one economy being formed on top of
a previous economy in our history, although we may not have
recognized the process. Look what the economy brought on by
the automobile (and trucks and highways) did to the railroads in
this century.

From the '60s to the '80s, our huge entrepreneurial revolution
looked a lot like the one at the turn of the century, which was
dominated by the automobile and the assembly line. This one has
developed an entirely new complexion dominated by inventions like
the microprocessor. John Naisbitt has said that we are fundamentally moving from an auto-driven economy to a computer-driven
economy. Who's to argue?

Now let's tie up a final point in the industry-economy-generation
relationship. To do that we introduce a new tool.

The Industry Life Cycle

Here's the classic four-stage model of the whole economy. Everything we talked about earlier comes together in Figure 6-3.

In this figure, the dark, labeled curve in the foreground is the four-stage Industry Life Cycle. The two generations that form this cycle are represented by the pair of smaller S-Curves in the background. The Individualist generation's Innovation Wave coincides with the Innovation Wave of the cycle. Radical innovations move into the mainstream with the Individualist generation's Spending Wave, causing a steep, exciting growth boom, which I refer to as a barroom brawl.

Next comes the transition from the Individualist generation to the Conformist generation. This transition occurs as a shakeout between the generations. More on shakeouts later.

For now, it's enough to know that the Conformist generation improves upon the radical innovations of Individualists with incremental innovation. For example, the Bob Hope generation ex-

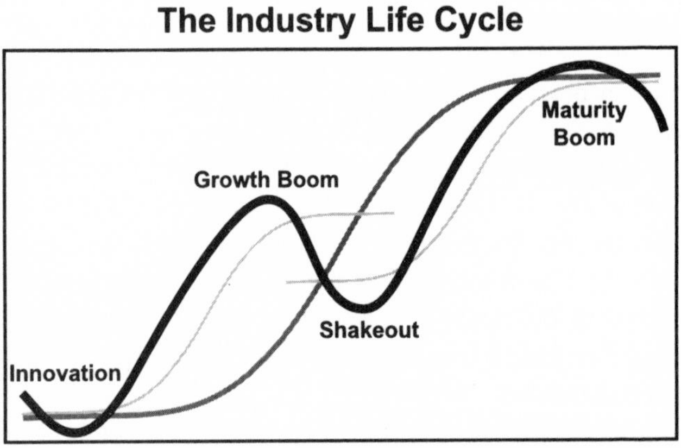

The Industry Life Cycle

Figure 6-3. The classic Industry Life Cycle

tended the radical innovation of the auto with all the power options and superhighways to drive them on.

Finally, the Spending Wave of Conformists coincides with a more gradual, more prolonged maturity boom, which I call the ballroom dance. The Bob Hope generation's maturity boom, begun in the '50s and '60s, can be attributed to this process. To finish my description of Figure 6-2, the single, larger S-Curve represents the Standardized Economy.

The point is that we've been transitioning into a new Customized Economy as this process has begun to be repeated. The Individualist baby boom generation with its radical innovations in microcomputers has been through its Innovation Wave. The baby boomer Spending Wave that will continue from about 1994 to 2010 will comprise the growth boom, the greatest in history because it's the largest so far.

Let's examine how clusters of technology move through the four stages of their Industry Life Cycles, forming a new economy.

Stage 1: Innovation—
the Innovation Wave of the
Individualist generation

The efficiencies made possible by the assembly line allowed hundreds of innovations to ultimately move with their companion generation into the mainstream of the economy, following the predictable paths of S-Curves.

When the Standardized Economy had its raw beginnings in the late 1800s, the automobile, electrical energy, and the telephone were invented. These basic innovations paved the way for an explosive entrepreneurial revolution that centered on the early 1900s.

I was struck when I learned that nearly all of the mass-market brand-name products we take for granted today did not exist before the turn of the century. While reading a book called *Entrepreneurs,*

I realized that the great majority of such products became commercial innovations around the first decade of this century. Look at Figure 6-4 to see just how productive and innovative the last individualist or entrepreneurial generation was.

These products and brand names—Campbell's soups, Coca-Cola, Hershey bars, Wrigley's chewing gum, Lipton's tea, disposable razor blades, electricity, elevators (which made skyscrapers feasible), and a host of our current mass-market products—were invented near the turn of the century as entrepreneurial businesses.

Clusters of Major Brand Innovations

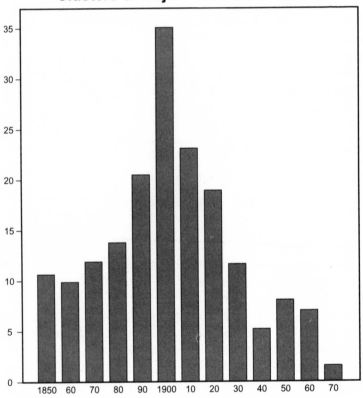

Figure 6-4. Launching dates of present major brand names
Source: *Entrepreneurs*, Joseph and Suzy Fuchini

A new economy emerges as the old is maturing, a process seen as a battle between the old and the new. It's a tug-of-war between the older generation and the products of the new. The Henry Ford generation led off the Innovation phase of the Standardized Economy. Today, the comparable innovation period from the late '60s to the early '80s has been launched by baby boomers. This generation has obviously been in conflict with the Bob Hope generation.

The values of the two successive generations always contend as new technologies supplant the old. More and more, new technologies go into new products and services to create new benefits in them. This period is nearly always characterized by inflation, the economy's way of financing the transition from the old technologies to the new, from one economy to the other. Low productivity usually results from the combination of new technologies being in their early learning phases and old technologies beginning to slow and falter.

Radical innovations come in. Although these innovations are first applied to improving old products and technologies, their real purpose is to set a new direction in the industry.

We're coming out of a similar stage now. Today's microcomputer technology, comparable to the automobile of the early part of the century, is multiplied in its potential by powerful, flexible software. This software, when married to hardware, can revolutionize any industry—just as the assembly line revolutionized industries throughout our economy in the last century in America.

This helps explain the '70s and '80s with their high inflation and radical innovations—those times were comparable to the early 1900s, the innovative years of automobiles, also a period of rising inflation.

So that's how the Innovation Wave of the Individualist generation causes a period of radical innovation, restructuring of old industries, and launching of new ones—creating inflation to finance this transition and incorporating the new generation into the work force.

Stage 2:
The growth boom—the Spending Wave
of the Individualist generation

Here's the time when innovations begin moving out of the niches into the mainstream, driven by the spending power of the Individualist generation. With their declining costs and higher productivity, these innovations eliminate the inflation of the past phase. During this period the old and the new fight over the new markets that will be dominating the economy. The Henry Ford generation's growth boom peaked in the Roaring Twenties, sparked by the efficiencies of the assembly line. A growth boom, generated by the Spending Wave of the Individualist generation, is wholly different in character from the maturity boom of the Conformist generation. In the growth boom you have numerous competitors racing for high-margin, fast-growth products that are moving rapidly into the mainstream, overtaking old industries. The coming growth boom from 1994 to 2010 will continue to exhibit the wild nature that we saw for a time in the '80s.

Surprisingly, because of conflicting forces, prices tend to remain relatively stable in such a period. New technologies put downward pressure on prices, but rising consumer demand from the Spending Wave exerts an upward pressure. The result? Stable prices while supply and demand are in balance. And this means favorable margins for businesses. That's why inflation stays low. I repeat—we will *not* see significant inflation in the coming growth boom!

America is entering just such a baby boomer growth boom. At the top of this boom in the 2000s, new industry leaders will emerge. There will be a lot of investments made toward building up capacity in this race. This buildup among so many competitors leads to excess capacity. So when the generation that spawns that first growth boom period stops spending—as the Henry Ford generation did around 1929 and the baby boom generation will around 2006 to 2010—the economy and all the new industries naturally

slip into the next phase, an across-the-board shakeout we know
as a depression.

Stage 3:
Shakeout, a time of depression—
the Innovation Wave of the
Conformist generation

This is a period of reckoning for the excesses that develop in the
growth boom. As they prosper, industries invest far too much in
building capacity in the race for leadership in growth markets.
Therefore, when consumer demand drops predictably after the
peak of the Individualist generation's Spending Wave, the economy
is left with a pool of excess capacity. Price wars result from everybody dumping product at lower prices. A shakeout occurs, leading
to the survival of the fittest. Only strong companies with the greatest economies of scale and brand loyalties will survive these times.
This shakeout process results in layoffs and bankruptcies, which
generate persistently high levels of unemployment and deflation in
prices. Depressions occur at a very specific time in the industry
cycle. They can be predicted, and even tempered, but not pre-
vented.

As this shakeout is occurring, another generation's innovations
begin to take shape. Technologies add incremental innovations to
the original, radical innovations of Individualists. The next generation comes along in its youth and innovates again. This time it's
the Conformist generation. Its incremental innovative efforts help
extend products into broader applications, creating the new growth
markets of the next boom. Besides giving us the power options
on cars, the Bob Hope generation improved the performance of
aircraft by the addition of jet engines. They also added automatic-
cycle washing machines and dryers and other home appliances that
increasingly liberated women from much of their everyday house-
work. It's these new incremental innovations that become the

growth markets of the maturity boom as each industry moves into mass markets.

If you're in business, the secret to success once you know when a depression will occur is to prepare for it, to maintain or increase market share, to spot the new incremental innovations, and to be ready to bounce back and grow in the most lucrative areas once the hard times are over.

Stage 4:
The maturity boom—
the Spending Wave of the
Conformist generation

In a maturity boom new growth segments gradually saturate the marketplace, so just about everybody who could possibly own the products reinnovated by Conformists will have them.

The handful of competitors left from the shakeout don't compete wildly. They keep reducing prices and promoting, but the industry is much more mature and stable.

The final chapter in this cycle is saturation and the peaking of that economy. As a new economy emerges in the next inflationary, innovation phase to follow the maturity boom, the old economy shrinks into another consolidation period, in which the big firms that dominate the market shake out even further. Old industry leaders are forced to meet competition from the new faces in the game. Even some of the old industry leaders will go under in the downturn following the maturity boom.

That's how it works. To summarize: An economy takes two generations to build. The last Standardized Economy was formed by the Individualist Henry Ford generation, which brought us the radical innovations led by the automobile. The Conformist Bob Hope generation brought incremental innovations to the original innovations. Now that economy is coming to an end.

The baby boom generation is the Individualist generation with microcomputers and related innovations. They will be followed by the Conformist Millennial generation, which will provide the incremental innovations that re-form the Customized Economy in the downturn from about 2010 to 2025, bringing technologies that will allow growth through mass customization in the maturity boom from around 2022 into the 2040s. For now let's look at the traits of the baby boom generation that are forming the basis of the new Customized Economy.

Inner-directed traits of baby boomers shaping the next economy

Certain individualistic and entrepreneurial characteristics differentiate baby boomers from their parents. They will be the factors that determine where new opportunities for entrepreneurship and growth will be created in the new economy.

However, the baby boom generation is individualistic in the extreme. And their character is multiplied by the incredible power of their innovations, based on microcomputer technology. Before the advent of microtechnologies, a customized or truly individualistic economy was not possible. Now it is inevitable.

In a nutshell here are the baby boomers . . .

Traits of the Baby Boom Generation
- Knowledgeable, informed buyers
- Quality conscious
- Highly participatory and experiential
- High discretionary income
- Convenience-oriented
- Highly individualistic
- Strive for self-improvement and perfection
- Value leisure and creative pursuits
- Conscious of health and environment

- Self-help-oriented
- Highly experimental
- Value passion, care, and the personal touch

Let's look at each trait in brief.

Knowledgeable, informed buyers
Baby boomers know what they want. They read labels, check with experts and friends, and conduct research before making a purchase. They rely on experience, word of mouth, and various consumer reports. For this reason, educational advertising and packaging directed at communicating the character of a product are becoming more critical in marketing.

Quality conscious
Yes, the yuppie baby boomers are status conscious, particularly those moving up social and career ladders. But most in that generation show more concern for the value of a well-made product, whether they are buying it or producing it. They know quality means durability, less maintenance, ease of operation, and effectiveness that gives greater satisfaction. Baby boomers have proven they will pay more for products like luxury import cars that prove to have a tangible quality trade-off in comparison to lower-priced domestic models.

Highly participatory and experiential
They want to receive something more than material satisfaction from products and services. They want to learn or experience something new or unique. They want to interact with a product or service, and it must be flexible enough to allow modification or customization. That's why interactive games, video, and other forms of flexible software, particularly software that's user-friendly enough to be customized, are so popular with baby boomers. Baby boomers aren't afraid to avoid a package tour so they can stay in a remote hotel to experience the local culture.

High discretionary income
Baby boomers, whether because of high earning power, or two careers in the family, or fewer

children, or fewer fixed obligations, have more money to spend on things other than necessities. This means that they can afford quality and that they will value many of the experiential pleasures like gourmet dining and travel.

Convenience-oriented   Baby boomers value convenience and conserve time for the same reasons. They want to make more time for the leisure and special-interest pursuits of importance to them. The company that can save them time and reduce life's struggles will get their business, even at a premium price. You don't have to be a visionary to see that in the past consumer demand for convenience has made successes of firms like Domino's Pizza and Federal Express.

Highly individualistic   Baby boomers seek their own life-styles. They expect a real choice in products and services and will pay a premium price to companies willing to customize to satisfy their needs. They prefer choices that serve their own productivity in their own work, specialty, or recreational areas. Unlike the Bob Hope generation, whose work ethic was for somebody, mainly men, to have a good job in any area so long as the family could be supported, baby boomers seek careers in their areas of personal interest and expertise.

Strive for self-improvement and perfection   Inner-directed baby boomers strive to know their strengths and weaknesses. They work to improve on both. They do so on the basis of their own standards of achievement and values. All types of new products oriented toward specialized learning, health, fitness, relationships, and communication will continue to grow rapidly. In these areas especially, baby boomers prefer the very best in quality. Likewise, they demand jobs in which they can grow and learn.

Value leisure and creative pursuits   Don't be fooled about baby boomers. They do work hard. After all, they were willing to put both wife and husband into the work force just to keep up with inflation. As a general rule, though, they are not content *only* to work hard. They want their work and leisure to be meaningful and self-expressive. They want balance in their lives. Studies of baby boomers have shown that they tend to spend an inordinate amount of time and money on a few key hobbies or interests. This makes them highly quality-sensitive in these areas. Often they can be highly price-sensitive in other areas, which they subordinate to their primary interests.

Conscious of health and environment
Quality of life is important to baby boomers. That means they prefer living and working in environments that are aesthetically pleasing and not just functional. A whole array of new or modified health and fitness products is growing around people's individualized health needs and concerns. The market for all types of industrial processes for cleaning up the environment is growing as stricter environmental laws are passed over time. Believe me, the recent minor relaxations in environmental laws due to the recession are a short-term aberration.

Self-help-oriented
As consumers, baby boomers want products that can be adapted to their own real and perceived needs. They shy away from pat answers and institutionalized approaches to problems. They are skeptical of institutions and despise bureaucracies. They prefer self- or home-diagnostic products and services. In the work arena they want to have more latitude to make their own decisions.

Highly experimental
The confidence of knowing what they want and what they value gives baby boomers more freedom to look at options, even if their choices do not fit the accepted norm. By making such individual choices, inner-directed people are the ones who initially give credibility to new products and services. They also are most likely to innovate new products and services. The ideal of most baby boomers is to run their own business.

Value passion, care, and the personal touch
This is an area in which business seems to have the most trouble adapting

to the values of baby boomers. Inner-directed people won't tolerate being treated inhumanely or insensitively, either as consumers or as workers. As John Naisbitt said in *Megatrends,* people today are requiring more of the "human touch" as a balance to the intrusion of technology and the level of enormous changes around them. And as Paul Hawken states, baby boomers will only give up their time and energy for something meaningful to them.

What does this all mean?

- **First, it means a new consumer** with increasingly powerful spending influence is creating a market in which many different products and services can only succeed by adapting to that consumer. Some segments will continue to demand the lowest prices or the best values. Other segments will demand the best quality, even at premium prices. Baby boomers will discriminate between products that really matter to them and those that do not.
- **Second, the new values** of the largest generation in history will create an entirely new means of achieving higher productivity in the workplace—tapping into the creative passions of self-directed workers. People will perform beyond the call of duty only when they can create and direct their own work and specialize in skills and causes that are meaningful to them.
- **Third, managers** who try to get their employees to fit into command and control systems will have problems. They will be incapable of keeping up with the productivity and innovation of firms that know how to motivate and reward the new worker.
- **Fourth, the inner-directed trends and deep social changes** that baby boomers bring with them will reward the individuals and companies that learn to take advantage of them in the great boom to come. Those that do not adapt to baby boomers will fall farther and farther behind as the old values move from the majority to the minority and become—sorry, Mom—irrelevant.

What it means is that the baby boom generation will absolutely determine the character of the new Customized Economy! And not just
the consumer sector of that economy. Every sector from industrial to
service to the strictly business-to-business companies will be forced
to embrace customization.

The characteristics of the Customized Economy

Driven by computer technology, the new economy will be giving
us an entirely new, entirely welcome flavor to our lifestyles.

Quality. You'll see much higher quality in and value added to
the products you buy. At long last you'll see, not merely adequate
products, but products that function in a superior manner. They
will be better designed to last longer and to create better results.
You're going to like this new economy, especially when you find
that quality will become increasingly affordable.

Customization. The new economy will address individual
needs. Products will be more precisely fitted to the tasks we
buy them for. Best of all, you'll have choices. Want a variety of
colors, styles, models, relative quality, and performance? You're
going to get them. You will eventually even be able to custom-
design your own house in a simulated three-dimensional environment where you get to see and experience your house before
you sign on the dotted line.

Fast response and delivery. In these days of sudden change
and high technology, time is the critical commodity. Customers,
whether business or consumer, cannot afford to wait for your
company to batch up products and run a big run and ship. People
like you who are planning in the here and now want results with

the same kind of speed. Businesses will learn to respond quickly . . . no, make that immediately, wherever possible. **Personalized, front-line service.** Expect to be treated as human beings and individual ones at that. The companies that will excel in the new economy will be forced to deliver respect and courtesy. Companies that fail to develop a sense that people must be dealt with as though they were possessed of individual personalities will fail to develop.

On a larger scale, every industry can increase its growth by adding higher value to its products and getting more customized features and more responsive services to the products already in use. The winning companies in America will be those that outcustomize the foreign competition. Forget trying to outstandardize them. That can no longer be done.

The United States leads the world in customizing technology made possible by the flexibility of computers and software. Hear me, folks, whatever we suffer from in the hardware department is made up many times over by our advantages in software. Our program applications will drive our jobs and machines and everybody else's in the foreseeable future—just as our dominance in television and movies drives social and fashion trends. We must start appreciating our strengths and seizing the new opportunities, rather than bemoaning the loss of certain standardized industries to foreign competitors. We will, in fact, regain leadership in many basic industries ranging from semiconductors to steel when those industries come to be dominated by customization and smaller-scale processes like mini-mills in steel.

The coming growth boom

Where are we going? Look where we've been. The previous generation owned the maturity boom, which peaked in the late '60s. This Bob Hope generation was more civic-minded, more conformist than either the Henry Ford generation before it or the baby boomers who are following. After the individualistic Roaring Twenties boom, when society seemed so fragmented, alienated by government, prohibition, and the adoption of the automobile, which put wheels under families, fragmenting society, people begin to say, "Enough of this individualism. How can we pull together?"

That generation became institution builders. They took the growth companies of the 1920s and turned them into major mass-market corporations. They were more scientific- and technology-minded. They tended to control and synthesize, making things tie together. They used the command and control leadership style they acquired in the services while fighting World War II. They innovated more at a technocratic level as opposed to a social level.

And now the global economy belongs to the largest generation in history. So it is inevitable that baby boomers will be taking us into the greatest boom in history.

A chart of the future economy

Figure 6-5 is perhaps the decisive graph in this book.

As best as I can depict any complex concept in a single graph, this one shows the relative size and strength of the two economies. Notice the relationship of the two generations that form each of these economies. From this figure you can get an idea of just how dramatic will be the upswing in the Customized Economy.

Since the '70s we've been in a shakeout caused by the change-over from the Standardized Economy to the Customized Economy. The recession of the early '90s was also affected by the shakeout of the baby boom Spending Wave as it moves from the growth boom phase to the maturity phase. But these shakeouts are nearly at an end.

America is going to lead the world into this global Customized Economy. The boom will be more dramatic than any previous one because the generation driving it is so large and their numbers are multiplied by the unprecedented power of their information technology and microtechnologies.

The Customized Economy Replacing the Standardized Economy

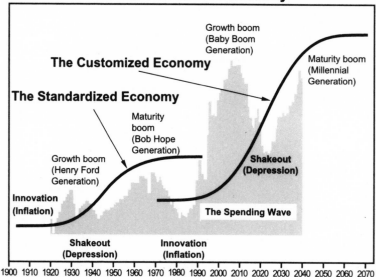

Growth boom
(Baby Boom
Generation)

The Customized Economy

Maturity boom
(Millennial
Generation)

The Standardized Economy

Maturity
boom
(Bob Hope
Generation)

Growth boom
(Henry Ford
Generation)

**Shakeout
(Depression)**

**Innovation
(Inflation)**

The Spending Wave

**Shakeout
(Depression)**

**Innovation
(Inflation)**

1900 1910 1920 1930 1940 1950 1960 1970 1980 1990 2000 2010 2020 2030 2040 2050 2060 2070

Figure 6-5. Integrating the Spending Wave with the S-Curves of the Standardized and Customized Economies

Based on the material we've covered so far, we're now able to construct a forecast for the global economy. That's the subject of our next chapter. There we'll see how the world is going to shape up in the coming boom. In Part II we'll examine the new growth markets that will be formed, permitting new opportunities. And we'll study the strategies for capitalizing on those markets.

PART II

HOW TO PROFIT IN THE GROWTH BOOM OF THE 1990S

*Strategies for exploiting
the Greatest Boom
in History*

Part II is for everybody too.

This section contains a thorough discussion of the strategies smart managers, owners, and entrepreneurs can be expected to employ in the coming new economy.

But I like to think of this section as critically important to everybody. You need to be able to spot S-Curves, social trends, and the principles that underlie all change, no matter how complex. You need the information to be able to answer questions like: Which companies should I invest in? What jobs should I take? What companies should I be in? Will I be among the also-rans or on the leading edge?

Most of all, you need to have the information that will help you make the right decisions in the coming boom. I hope you'll find Part II a kind of mini-MBA that will lead you where you need to go, even if business and management are not your main areas of interest. These principles and this knowledge will be valuable to anyone.

7

The Global Boom
Scenario

*A New World Economic
Order on the horizon*

BULLETIN

Japan will be slow to recover from its tumble into the world's economic cellar. Europe will stagger under the burden of restructuring the former Soviet bloc and Eastern Europe for years to come. The United States, with its huge baby boom and its edge in customizing technologies and entrepreneurial skills, will enjoy a head start in the drive to dominate the global economy, especially if it forms the right partnerships.

Three trading blocs reshape
the global economy

All the predictive tools point to prosperity. Spending Waves, Innovation Waves, technology S-Curves, the S-Curve of the customized economy, and inflation's end indicate a booming world economy originating in the United States by the second half of 1994. The trends also clearly point to a dramatic restructuring into a New World Economic Order with three major trading blocs. North America, led by the United States, will be the strongest. A European bloc will be moving into a competitive second position over the coming decades. A Far Eastern bloc will likely be less cohesive at first and continue to grow but will be limited by economic difficulties in Japan and its competition with rising Third World countries like Mexico and Eastern Europe.

As the recession progresses in 1993, you can expect to see rising tensions. Look for protectionist tendencies to continue to grow, among individual nations within each bloc, but particularly among the major blocs: Japan and the Far East, Europe, and North America. This very tendency toward protectionism in tough economic times is likely to strengthen the trend toward the formation of trading blocs as geographic neighbors gravitate toward each other.

Despite the European Community's recent thrust toward an integrated Europe, petty infighting has compromised the movement. And it will probably continue to be slow until after this recession when the strong resurgence of the United States motivates closer economic integration among the countries within each bloc. Why is this so? First, the difficulties in the Soviet Union and Eastern Europe have proven to be so complex. Second, the worsening recession continues to promote strong feelings of nationalism within and among countries. This is a polarizing force just at the time the economic community was supposed to come together. So I expect Europe to come out of the recession either slower or later than the United States. It might be more like 1995 or later before European countries begin to exhibit their economic luster again.

The recession will at first reduce U.S. willingness to integrate with Canada and Mexico as an economic bloc. In the 1992 campaigns of both political parties you'd have been deaf not to hear the appeals to restrict trade with Mexico and other countries. That tactic of playing to people's fears always crops up in tough times.

But as the United States moves strongly out of this recession, the fear of losing jobs overseas and calls for protectionism will diminish quickly. The United States will likely be the first country to make strong overtures toward its neighbors to form a meaningful economic trading bloc. Meanwhile, the Europeans will probably continue to debate their nationalistic differences. The Europeans will awaken to reality, though. They'll realize they have to stop arguing when the United States and the North American trading bloc starts expanding its share of world markets at their expense as individual countries.

The success of the North American bloc will finally motivate the European Economic Community to get serious and aggressive about economic cooperation and integration. When they finally do, they will become the largest integrated marketplace of consumers in the world.

The Far East trading bloc will likely be the slowest to integrate economically. The economic shock to Japan will create somewhat of a void in leadership in the Far East—and Japan was never liked that much there anyhow. Countries like Korea, Taiwan, and Singapore have more trade with the United States than with Japan. We may even see some of these Far Eastern countries attempting to integrate with the North American bloc, leaving no clear trading bloc in the Far East. So that region may, like Eastern Europe, represent an arena of political rivalry and military unrest for the coming years.

A look at the size and timing of generations in each potential trading bloc shows how they will unfold.

The Generation Wave Without a doubt, the United States and Canada have the largest relative baby boom generations coming into their peak spending and productivity years. Their Spending Wave began surging in 1982. It will resume its momentum even more powerfully in 1994 and continue out to 2006 to 2010, causing the greatest consumer spending impetus in the world to occur in North America. Figure 7-1 shows how the North American Spend-

A Comparison of Global Baby Booms

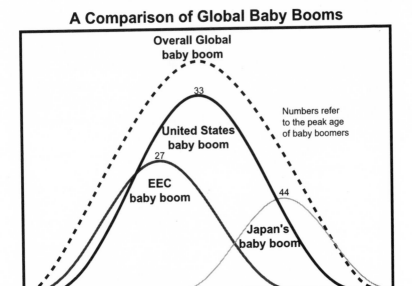

Figure 7-1. The relationship between the baby booms of the
world's economic leaders to date

ing Wave of that generation will be much stronger than Europe's,
and far, far stronger than Japan's, which will be turning downward
in the last half of the '90s.

This figure shows the relative timing and size of baby boom
generations of Europe, the United States, and Japan. Clearly, the
United States had a far larger baby boom than either Europe or
Japan. Canada's demographics are parallel to our own, adding to its
power. Notice the discrepancy in peak ages of the various booms.
In our country, the peak of the baby boom is about age 33 today.
The Spending Wave of a generation peaks in spending around age
49, so we have a good 16 years of boom ahead for our economy.

Contrast that with Japan, whose baby boomers are already beginning to peak in their Spending Wave. They had a smaller generation that peaked in births just after World War II, many years
ahead of the United States. After their devastating defeat and

demoralizing destruction by atomic weapons, it simply was not an optimum time for births. So the peak of the Japanese baby boom generation is about age 44 right now—well near the peak of the Spending Wave and past the all-important peak for housing at age 43. This means Japan's Spending Wave will be peaking between 1990 and 1997. So their consumer economy will be weakening in the late '90s and early 2000s just as the United States enters the strongest leg of its consumer boom. This is another reason I feel Japan will be slow to recover from the recession and will be a weaker contender in the world economic race in the future.

Incidentally, if you looked farther ahead into the future, you would see a different story. Because the Japanese had a second baby boomlet, which will be in a rising phase of spending between about 2010 and 2025, they'll enjoy prosperity while we will be on the decline again. In fact, this generation will be more creative and individualistic and most probably improve upon our Customized Economy the way their last generation improved upon our Standardized Economy.

Birth trends in Europe lagged behind those of the United States because of the time it took to recover from the destruction of World War II. So Europe's baby boom is younger—with a peak age of about 27—and also a smaller baby boom than that of the United States. All along we have seen the tendency for Europe's economy to boom and bust later than that of the United States. We have seen the European entrepreneurial revolution lag about six years behind ours because of this difference. So the good news for Europe is that their economy will peak later than ours, around 2015 to 2016, allowing for the varying age demographics in the different countries of Europe.

The dotted line in Figure 7-1 represents an approximation of the overall worldwide baby boom. It's clear that the global boom in births is centered on that of North America. So the global economy is going to follow the performance of the United States and Canada as well.

What about the retirement numbers?

During the coming boom Japan and Germany will have substantially higher retirement populations in proportion to their working populations than the United States. Our economy will be dominated by the higher productivity of the baby boomers, who will far outweigh the burden of higher numbers of retirees.

Demographic trends say that the retirement population will grow more slowly in the coming decade than in the past one. We've already seen the smaller Bob Hope generation fully enter retirement in the 1980s. The retirement population will only grow moderately in the next decade from the fact that life expectancies are continuing to extend out. Baby boomers won't enter retirement until after the boom, the leading edge of the generation arriving at age 65 at the peak of this boom.

Of course, the positive effects enormous baby boom numbers will have on the coming boom will be reversed in spades after its peak. Baby boomers will deepen the depression that follows around 2010, first because they will have peaked in their spending, which causes the economy to tail off. And second because baby boomers will start entering their unproductive years of retirement, causing a severe drag on the economy.

So much for demographics and the Spending Wave. Let's look at the coming boom in the light of another, more critical factor favoring the North American bloc.

The Customized Economy   Despite the ground we lost to Japan in the '70s and '80s in efficiencies of the Standardized Economy, we're moving into an increasingly global Customized Economy in which flexibility and creativity will be the decisive factors. Based on computers and software, the leader going in is clearly the United States. The United States will be the biggest beneficiary of the trend toward customization and the microcomputer revolution. Because the world economy is moving away from their strengths, Japan is going to benefit least. Will they try to leapfrog from the standardized to the customized? Sure they will. Can they do it without their money machine and with a less than creative population? Probably not. At least not until their second mini-baby boom, which is likely to be more creative, comes into their Spending Wave ten to fifteen years from now. Here's how the three blocs stack up.

Japan and the Far East. Customization is not the game for the Japanese. Individuality is discouraged in their culture. In fact, for that reason, their highly prized education system will work to their disadvantage in the Customized Economy. They have rarely excelled as entrepreneurs or in businesses that require a large degree of customization and specialization. Their people are not trained to think for themselves or to make their own decisons in their vaunted education system. The microcomputers they do have are not in consumer hands or even worker hands—they're in company hands.

What's more, the Japanese primarily dominate the standardized hardware markets that are going to be declining faster in the '90s. Just as Japan outstandardized the United States, they are going to have increasing competition from the so-called Four Tigers—Korea, Taiwan, Singapore, and Hong Kong. These Third World countries pulled themselves up through industrialization to become Second World countries in the last decade. Korea, Taiwan, Singapore, and Hong Kong generally have booming Spending Waves more in line with that of the United States. Already they have proven themselves to be capable competitors. Look at Korean automobiles moving into American markets today. It's hard to avoid comparisons with the original tinny Japanese cars of decades ago. As Japan's sun sinks, the more favorable age demographics and less troubling economic situations of other countries on the Pacific Rim will continue to fill the vacuum.

Korea has a clear strategy of overtaking Japan in the region, doing to Japan what it has done to others. We can expect an ongoing joust for regional leadership. With no clear military or political leadership in the area, the contest might remain unsettled for some time to come. One thing is certain—an almost universal dislike of Japan exists. Whether this dislike stems from World War II (and imperialism that even predates that) or whether this is another case of get-even, or merely an instance of pure, healthy, aggressive competitiveness, look for an economic struggle that is sure to keep the region fragmented for a long time.

> If a Pacific Rim leader does emerge further down the line to succeed Japan, my feelings are that it will stem from the growing region of China from Hong Kong to Guangdong Province. What I like about this region is that it's a real grass-roots entrepreneurial area. In other words, its growth is not due to centralized government planning. In fact, they have flagrantly violated the policies of Beijing.

Even now the Communist Chinese government is holding them up as a prototype for China. And remember, 1997 is the year Hong Kong reverts from British to Chinese control.

In the long term, China is a huge country with a lot of potential. But with all its backward conditions and the centralized, decrepit government, it will take many more decades to move into world competition. But the Chinese can do it by expanding the model of Hong Kong–Guangdong over time. I predict China will eventually become a world leader, beginning as early as 2040, in the Customized Economy or the economy that succeeds it.

However, with all that said, the Pacific Rim will not be the dramatic growth engine it has been in the last two decades.

> In complete contrast to traditional predictions, my forecasting tools indicate that the consensus that says we're moving to a Pacific Rim–dominated world is totally wrong. The brief phenomenon of Pacific Rim preeminence won't resurface with staying power for many decades to come. Instead, in the next two decades we will increasingly see a return to an Atlantic Rim economic focus as the United States and North America lead in economic growth and Europe becomes the next most competitive bloc as the boom progresses.

Europe. If you read the books out there, people are telling you, "Europe is going to overtake the United States—the EEC will be the largest, most competitive marketplace in the world." No way—for now, Europe still has integration problems—those countries are not going to come together overnight and agree on everything. Eastern Europe and Russia are going to require many years of patience and restructuring before the dividends are paid back from the heavy investments there. Germany's capital will be drained by the depression and painful restructuring process in Eastern Europe and the former Soviet republics—far more than they bargained for. Western Europe must make a large investment and have the patience to wait for them to change to a truly market economy from their former controlled economies.

Europe comes out good in my analysis for the future but not so great in the near-term scenario. I expect Europe's strong competitive surge to come toward the latter end of this boom—in the late '90s and early 2000s. Yes, Europe has a tradition of quality, customization, and targeting of high-end, specialty markets. But several factors work against Europe in the boom.

The Achilles' heel of most European countries is they don't have the modern technologies for efficient production that the Japanese and the United States increasingly have. Of course, there are many exceptions to that statement. And they are behind in the entrepreneurial and microtechnology strengths of the United States for competing efficiently in the more customized markets. Europe still has a high degree of central planning and socialism in many countries. Such systems tend to minimize taking risks as they rely on "good old boy" networks of competition that aren't so "good" in the information age. Entrepreneurs must take risks to get an edge—otherwise, they will stay in the midst of the slow-moving pack. This is not to say that every country must have a free-market system exactly like the United States. But the countries that lean toward true free-market economies are going to have the advantages in the faster pace of the customized world and the information age.

One more factor works against Europeans. They have a tendency toward a craftsman mentality that plays down process and technology in favor of the master craftsman. How can they catch up to the technology of Japan for production and the United States for customization and service for the mass market? Again, without help, they won't.

North America. The United States will come screaming out of this recession. If the right strategies are followed, it will suddenly be obvious to the rest of the world that the strongest trading bloc potential in the world lies in North America.

Of course, the road is not without obstacles. The United States will have to overcome its minority of isolationist factions. And, of course, you can't expect policies that will shift jobs to Mexico to be supported during the recession. However, after the recession we must become aggressive at building cooperation, integrating Mexico as the partner with a low-cost production center and Canada as the partner with a highly skilled work force and a natural resource base to complement our own. We can extend our trading bloc and sphere to countries in the Far East and South America as well, over time, if we are smart. If that happens, North Americans, with their burgeoning baby boom market and the microcomputer revolution with so many customized technologies moving into the mainstream, will clearly dominate the global economy.

The United States has the greatest advantage with consumers in specialty markets. We dominate in the technologies that count in the coming Customized Economy. We dominate in television and software. We dominate in communications and microcomputers—all kinds of customized products and services. That's what we're good at—despite declining SAT scores among baby boomers for years.

We have to question whether these old instruments truly measure the factors that will count in the future. SAT scores primarily measure the left-brain skills like basic verbal and mathematical abilities that were so critical in the Standardized Economy. In the Customized Economy, right-brain and human skills will be more important.

Anybody wishing to return to the good old days of our prized education system of the past should consider this simple statistic I heard cited by an expert on innovation. He said that children typically lose 90 percent of their creative powers between the ages of five and seven after entering the rigid teaching environment of our school system. Most people today who are creative have had to spend years making readjustments from the education and bureaucratic systems that have suffocated them over the years. Most people now need therapy to reacquire some portion of their childhood creativity. Clearly, the Customized Economy will not tolerate an education system that values rote learning and memorization over creativity.

Having said that, I fully realize that past teaching models that rely solely on either discipline or creativity have run into problems of rigidity and permissiveness, respectively. Our education system must maintain discipline while fostering creativity. But this is being done successfully all over the country. Many of our leading-edge athletic and academic coaches have learned to combine creativity and discipline effectively. Many of our private schools and more progressive public schools have successfully proven that you can achieve creativity and discipline. Our challenge will be to incorporate these new prototypes throughout our public school system in the coming decades and to come up with new measurements that reflect creativity and right-brain skills as well as discipline and left-brain skills. These are the very skills that our own baby boom generation has pioneered—in particular, right-brain skills.

All this is generating opportunities for new products and services in the emerging Customized Economy. But here's the main point. The Japanese and Germans certainly might be raising more scientists and mathematicians than the number coming out of the American education system. But we have learned something different from what the Japanese have learned, something I feel is even more valuable. Our society has yet to learn to value and measure these new skills. And we, as a whole, are reluctant to recognize the possibility that the need for old skills has diminished. This is the wrong attitude to have. Think about it. Not so long ago in high school it was essential that math, chemistry, and physics students learn to use the slide rule for computing. Nowadays is there anybody in the United States still using a slide rule? Why would anybody do that when hand-held calculators are so much quicker, more powerful, and more accurate?

The microcomputer revolution is automating and making more accessible the basic verbal and mathematical skills of the past. The point is not that people shouldn't have basic skills but that advances in software and computers are going to make up for many liabilities. As computers provide us the powers to access and use them in a friendly manner, they will free up humans to focus on more consequential, creative, entrepreneurial, and human skills. That's just the kind of opening for which the United States has demonstrated the greatest aptitude. *And that's what will count in the coming Customized Economy!*

That said, I feel obliged to address head-on what many observers feel is the lowered educational background of people entering the work force in the next fifteen years. True, universal deficiencies in education could certainly dull our country's competitive edge. But our economic prowess is determined by its best-educated, not its worst-educated. Our energy derives from its most creative people, not its least inventive. With all its faults, we still have the best university and higher education system in the world. We have 75 percent of all the MBAs in the world. The challenge for our country will be for our higher-educated population to design software and systems that make our middle and lower sectors far more productive. So the effect of a small segment of our less-educated population won't be felt that much. For those who want it, job training and retraining will be available because the overall predicted shortages in labor will force businesses to offer it to upgrade the skills of those who didn't get what they needed from our education system. Finally, we have to face the reality that a certain small percentage of our population may be either beyond help or beyond even wanting it. The kinds of jobs they would be able to fill will be displaced by automation or the job requirement will be shipped to Mexico.

Let's look at the basic factors that demonstrate how the United States enjoys the competitive advantage in a Customized Economy.

We're the strongest player in the microcomputer revolution. If you listen to the press and traditional economists, you'll hear how our lack of a national industrial policy has given the Japanese and Germans the lead in establishing key technological infrastructures, such as fiber optics. Of course, the Japanese made the first concerted thrust at high-definition television with the help of its government. But a number of experts already claim that the Japanese moved too early into inferior analog technologies for HDTV.

Whether the Japanese erred or not, the fundamental point is this: our free-market economy and our more creative generation chose to focus on leading the most critical technologies driving the Customized Economy—not the ones driving the old Standardized Economy. We have been placing microcomputers, televisions, fax machines, VCRs, portable phones, and the best application software into the hands of entrepreneurs, workers, and consumers. Ours is a grass-roots system of creativity and innovation. That's the key factor in a Customized Economy.

Why don't our pessimistic economists who are bemoaning the loss of the Standardized Economy show you the statistics for the installed base of microcomputers in each country? In 1988, the installed base of microcomputers in the United States was 45 million. The rest of the world is not even in the ball game. Japan has about 5 million. Shouldn't this be considered a critical infrastructure? How are the Japanese going to become entrepreneurial and creative if their basic workers and consumers haven't learned how to use the most important tool of the Customized Economy, the personal computer?

How about microcomputers in Europe? The United Kingdom has fewer than 6 million—that's because they speak English and therefore have access to the best software in the world. Germany has about 5 million, about the same as Japan, but far behind the United States.

When you look at personal computers for each 100 inhabitants, the United States has more than 18. Canada is second with 11, and the United Kingdom has 10. Germany has 8.

Japan? Four—behind nearly every country in Europe except Italy.

Taiwan has 3, and South Korea only 0.5. Again, this points out the fact that as efficient as the Japanese are at assembly-line organizations, they don't have an orientation toward entrepreneurialism and individual use of personal computers.

Yes, Japan and Europe have made better investments than we have in certain broad-scale infrastructures, like fiber optics. But where is development going to happen? It's going to happen at the individual level. That's people with microcomputers who are entrepreneuring and serving customized companies. The United States has that infrastructure. We have all the basic tools for this new revolution—more cars, televisions, faxes, PCs, and VCRs per capita than any other country in the world. The fiber optic networks will and are clearly following the needs that will be generated by this grass roots revolution in microtechnologies.

We have the world's most flexible, creative workers. There is no question that our baby boom workers—now coming into their most productive years—are more creative than Europeans and far more creative than the Japanese. We have the best entrepreneurial sector in the world. We dominate almost every creative business segment, from television and music to computer software. Our creation of more than 20 million jobs in the 1980s has come from smaller, more entrepreneurial businesses, from which much of the creativity is spawned.

Our people may not be more disciplined or more systematic, but they are more inventive. That's what this new economy is going to demand. Working smart is going to mean more than working hard. Being able to customize and meet the needs of consumers will be more important than coming out with the lowest-cost vanilla product. Great as the Lexus and Infiniti are, they still come in only a handful of colors. And you want to mix and match options? Good luck.

In summary, in the year 2000, our greatest competition in the world market is likely to stem from Europe, and our greatest trade flow will be with Europe as well.

The transfer of wealth to
the Third World

To date, the Third World countries have depended on Japan, the
United States, and Europe as markets for selling oil, raw materials,
rice, sugar, coffee, tea, bananas, and such. That worked well
enough in the '70s because inflation kept prices up. In the '80s,
however, those countries did poorly because of deflation, which
dropped prices of their crops and natural resources. That deflation
was a signal to the Third World that they'd do better to get out of
commodities and to reshape their economies into an industrial format like that of Japan and the Four Tigers.

The question in the '90s will be: "Which Third World countries
actually will accomplish a move into the Industrial Age?" Mexico
is obviously well on track already. To relatively lesser degrees, in
the following approximate order, so are much of Eastern Europe,
Brazil, Argentina, parts of China, and the former Soviet Union.

> The resurgence of growth in the United States should make Mexico
> the Third World country with the strongest growth in the coming
> years.

Eastern Europe will take longer to emerge but we will see a
definite upturn in the industrialization curve starting with East Germany and spreading to Czechoslovakia, Hungary, and Poland,
roughly in that order. Investment in the former Communist states
and technological infusions will come primarily from Germany, but
also from other European countries and the United States. Sooner
or later, Russia and the former republics of the Soviet Union will
likewise eventually follow Eastern Europe into industrialization in
the second half of the '90s. The states that have the most potential

are the Ukraine, Russia, Kazakhstan, the Baltic states, and Georgia, again roughly in that order.

China will progressively expand its successful model of industrialization in Hong Kong and Guangdong to other provinces. Slowly but surely they will become the next superpower over the next century.

Can South America, Central America, and Africa get into the race to industrialize? To some degree, yes, but these countries will likely continue to be dominated by trade in raw materials and commodity products.

Many of the countries in North Africa will sooner or later be invited into the European Community trade bloc, which will give them an advantage over the more backward countries in central Africa.

In South America, Brazil, Argentina, Uruguay, and Paraguay have begun to integrate as an economic unit and to consolidate many of their industrial factions through joint ventures. Therefore we can expect this emerging South American bloc to eventually become another strong industrializing economy behind Mexico.

Finally, now that the polarization no longer exists between the United States and the former Soviet Union, Third World countries don't have to align with one side or the other. So Cuba is an example of how positive economic changes could now come to many of the smaller ex-Communist Third World countries.

In general, the worst of it for the Third World countries is over. Some Third World countries will be big beneficiaries of the boom that follows the global recession. Of course, they're not going to be able to leap to the Customized Economy. But I've already established that the economic superpowers can't afford to stay in the traditional Standardized Economy. Yet we will always need some products that can only be manufactured by standardized methods for the masses. That means . . .

The Third World will increasingly inherit the Standardized Economy, competing with Japan and Korea in standardized industrial goods and service. In fact, they will eventually dominate the Standardized Economy, forcing other industrial countries to move into the higher-value-added Customized Economy.

Now let's review the New World Economic Order and some of the strategies required for North America to enjoy maximum prosperity.

A New World Economic Order

The three major integrated economies will subcontract much of the standardized economy from the larger developed countries to Third World partners. Here's a brief rundown of how that will happen.

North America. As a robust economy and job growth return to the United States, our country will increasingly realize that its opportunities are in the higher-wage Customized Economy or in highly automated facets of the Standardized Economy. To the degree that we can compete at all in older industries, we will have to move aspects of production or assembly to Mexico. General Motors' and Ford's best automotive plants are there already. We are better off contracting standardized goods and components to Mexico rather than to the Far East. First, and most obviously, Mexico is closer. As we help Mexico industrialize we will increase their consumers' incomes. In turn that creates increased demand for higher-value products and services from our country—thus creating more and better jobs than we lose in the Standardized Economy. Canada, Mexico, and the United States will integrate as the most powerful global economic unit with secondary connections to South America, particularly countries like Brazil and Argentina.

Europe. The same logic will apply in Europe. Investments in and the subcontracting of standardized goods and components to Eastern Europe, North Africa, and the former Soviet Union will aid the former communist-bloc countries in their quest to compete as low-cost producers in world markets. And just think how it will create demand in those countries for finished goods and services from European countries. After all the deprivation suffered by former Soviet-bloc people under communism, they're a consumer explosion just waiting to happen.

Germany will be the key driving force in the integration with Eastern Europe, the former Soviet Union, and, secondarily, Africa and the Middle East. Germany will increasingly become the number two industrial power in the world, replacing Japan.

The Far East. The industrialized countries in the Far East will have to increasingly subcontract many components and products to countries like China to compete with countries in the other two blocs. Japan and Korea will develop markets in China and the countries of the Pacific Rim.

In each of these blocs, the main power will subcontract its industrial needs to the Third World countries in its geographical sphere. Trading will go on within the bloc and also with countries of other blocs.

Bottom-line strategies for the United States

The biggest winner in the world is destined to be the United States. Thus the biggest winner in the Third World is likely to be Mexico. Although many trends are in motion toward realizing that supremacy, it won't be totally automatic. No act of God or Mother Nature can do more than has already been done by the laws of economics and the overwhelming birth numbers coming together at a time of changeover from an old economy to a new. We have to have the good sense to recognize the unique circumstances before us. And we have to act, not waste our advantage bickering about the details of implementation while the rest of the world closes the gap on us. We can control our destiny in the coming boom. Which leads us to . . .

Strategy No. 1—Embrace our own advantages
Remember the Human Model of Forecasting from Chapter 2? I refer to it time and again because it describes so well our most telling shortcoming. We have this tendency to sacrifice long-term possibilities with a myopic preoccupation—if not an outright obsession—with what's happening today. We're sometimes our own worst enemy when it comes to taking action. No matter how ripe the moment, we seem to have groups in this country that will deliberate themselves into destruction.

We'll have the strongest market for customized goods and the skills required to produce them. So we should embrace the new Customized Economy as an opportunity that is supported by the jobs freed up by the departure of many old standardized industries.

You watch. We'll be staring at the immutable birth statistics that prove beyond any doubt that we will be faced with crippling labor shortages after this recession. These numbers are indisputable. Births are down in the post–baby boom years. That means we simply won't have the people to fill jobs in this unprecedented boom period. Yet there will be special interest groups arguing that we shouldn't invest in automation because it robs jobs and costs too much.

Strategy No. 2—Embrace Mexico
We'll have to accept Mexico as a true partner as we upgrade our own economy from the standardized to the customized.

By moving the standardized segment of our economy to Mexico, we do not lose jobs—that's a horribly short-term view. We gain big time in the long term by subcontracting work and moving jobs to Mexico. We'll be moving the lower-level jobs that nobody wants, freeing up our people to do higher-level jobs. Besides, while our baby boomers are reaching peak productivity, the follow-on generation is much smaller. We're going to be suffering from a shrinking labor force! It's going to become more obvious that, with the labor shortages and a growing market that we're dominating, we simply *must* subcontract work to Mexico or we won't be able to grow fast enough to keep up with the new economy.

Mexico will be only too happy to have jobs for its huge under-employed labor force. Higher Mexican incomes from their new jobs will allow them to buy more goods they can't produce themselves. They'll help the North American bloc compete in industries like autos—in the final assembly-line work that we're no longer good at.

There will be losers in the short term, but only in our high-paying, low-skill jobs—which we're destined to lose sooner or later anyhow. The greatest loss in wages and jobs in the '80s occurred not among minorities, but among high-school-educated white males. These sectors had in the past entered high-paying unionized jobs with relatively low skills in many standardized manufacturing industries. The message is clear: *If you have a job that's high paying and low skilled, you can expect to lose it to overseas competition or watch as it is automated.*

Although we will have the first opportunity to ally with Mexico, Japan—ever the competitor—will be saying, "Forget putting plants in the United States. Put them in Mexico." We should realize that by putting plants in Mexico we can save the more substantial remaining portion of many industries that we would otherwise lose to foreign competitors, as we lost them to Japan in the past. For example, in the auto industry, wouldn't it be better to transfer the assembly of automobiles to Mexico to ensure that we remain competitive and keep the much larger sectors of the industry from design to marketing to sales to service?

Strategy No. 3—Embrace Eastern Europe and Russia

The third most important thing we can do is preempt Germany somewhat by establishing an economic presence in Eastern Europe and the former Soviet Union republics.

Here we have some openings too. Although Germany has already indicated a major commitment and has invested capital to help fund their development, Eastern Europeans and Russians have natural fears from Germany's past. They want Germany's help, but they don't want to be dominated. Eastern Europeans also fear the Russians. This creates a political and business opportunity for the United States. Our government can offer an umbrella of military security and political support in exchange for mutual trade concessions and for open doors for business investments and joint ventures with U.S. companies.

> People who think our military dominance will be more of a strain than an advantage are missing the picture. It could be a huge advantage in establishing trade agreements with countries from Eastern Europe to the Far East to expand our marketplace in a world that is forming into more protective trade blocs.

The question is, will we capitalize on it? The question Richard Nixon raises—"Are we going to be asking who lost Russia?"—is a valid one. We must make it a high priority to establish our economic interests in Eastern Europe. Otherwise, economic dominance there is going to eventually go overwhelmingly to Europe and we're going to be locked out of one of the major growth areas and important consumer markets in the New World Economic Order.

In this age, when the United States surges back into global economic leadership, our biggest competitor will increasingly be

Europe. It will be a race. Will Europe dominate the development of Russia and Eastern Europe, or will the United States get its fair share? Europe obviously has the edge, but we will have a stronger position in the world if we grab some of that pie and don't let Europe totally dominate in Eastern Europe. After all, many Japanese and European companies are already setting up plants in Mexico.

Strategy No. 4—Joint venture with Europe The United States, already the strongest marketplace in the world and with the greatest natural advantages in the coming boom, has incredible leverage. That leverage allows us to say to other nations and multinational corporations, "If you want into our market, let's trade technologies or let us into your markets." It will give us the capacity to demand the formation of joint ventures. The New World Economic Order might just be one big joint venture at all levels— eventually eclipsing the power of national governments—but not for many decades to come. Each bloc has something unique to contribute to the party.

The Europeans realize they've got growing markets, quality products, and good design skills. But they won't have the low-cost production capability, except in certain German-dominated industries like chemicals. And they won't have the latest microcomputer technologies for customizing. So we're going to see European firms willing to enter into joint ventures with Japan for mass production technology and with the United States to gain microtechnologies for customized production.

The strategy is obvious. Either cooperate with European companies where possible or watch the Japanese do it. Somebody has to continue to beat the drum, so for now, it might as well be me. Whether because of all of our advantages and positioning, or merely because of our blessings or good luck, we're going to inherit the position of global economic leadership. We can either pick up the baton and run with it. Or we can drop it and eat the dust of the rest of the world. Do we really think the Japanese will be content to be also-rans? No, they will compete aggressively. Our choices allow for anything but to be isolationist and protectionist.

Strategy No. 5—Joint venture with Japan and the Far East After being set back in many international markets, Japanese firms are going to realize the only way to bounce back is through these same joint ventures. They'll be forced to face the reality that they can no longer bully their way in with their excess capital. So they're going to have to joint-venture with European and United States firms to keep some presence in the markets that are going to grow far better than theirs. It's going to put Japan in a different role. After looking like they were going to dominate the world economy, they will now have to settle more for positions as management, technological, and process consultants. The Japanese can also earn their way by joint-venturing with the countries that do have the markets.

The smarter American companies won't turn down joint ventures with the Japanese when they can manage our plants better for production than we can. If we're going to establish plants in Mexico, it may be best that we hire Japanese managers or subcontract with Japanese firms to set up and run those plants because they're often better at that than we are.

We should equally be targeting the emerging industrializing countries of the Far East like the Hong Kong–Guangdong areas for joint ventures and establishing footholds in such growth areas.

> We will see corporations in the United States, Europe, and Japan entering into more joint ventures that exchange capital, technologies, and market access. The real trend in the long term is the slow disappearance of the nation-state as an economic unit and the rise of large multinational corporations as the economic and even political entities of the world economy.

Somewhere in the future we may see the political and economic impact of these three trading blocs diminish, but for the near term their evolution and further integration seem inevitable—a necessary intermediate step to a true world economy with global free trade.

8

Investment Strategies for the '90s

*Putting your money where
the money will be*

BULLETIN

The past two decades favored investments that hedged against inflation—gold and real estate. But inflation will not be a factor in the coming new economy. So this new cycle will favor growth stocks and long-term bonds . . . provided you use the proper timing. You will need three distinct strategies for three key investment environments: 1993 to 1997, 1998 to 2006, and 2007 on.

That was then, this is now

The previous chapters outlined the forces underlying the economy. You know how those forces will affect the global economic scenario. You know which tools can be used to make predictions about the direction and timing of the economy. Now you want to know about your personal and business investments.

Here's a guiding principle. Let inflation (or its opposite number, deflation) determine how you invest. And my key point is that we won't have inflation in the foreseeable future.

The '70s and '80s, two past decades of inflation, favored investments like gold and real estate. You'd have done well to buy gold in the '70s and real estate in the '80s to maximize your investment potential. Gold appreciated both as a reaction to inflation and as a means of securing wealth against some of the crises in the world, the peak of the oil crisis and during the Iran hostage crisis, for example.

Real estate was a leveraged hedge against inflation, especially in the '80s. By leveraged, I mean it went up as fast as or faster than inflation—but you only bought it with 20 cents on the dollar, your down payment. So you were in a winning position, actually benefiting from inflation by owning a home or other real estate that appreciated—until real estate came back down to earth in the late '80s and early '90s.

Investments like gold and real estate will fall dramatically in 1993 and possibly into 1994. So let's discuss the here and now of deflation.

Remember that in the deflationary recession from 1980 to 1982, inflation went from 15 percent to 3 percent. When we came out of that recession, interest rates fell, prices dropped, consumers started spending, and we had an incredible boom from 1982 to 1986. That was the strongest part of the '80s boom.

Deflation is always negative at first because it squeezes weak businesses, causing a shakeout. Companies that can't compete in times of declining prices must fail. That results in unemployment and causes a deflationary recession. In fact, our worst recessions in history have been deflationary. The Great Depression was the worst ever.

However, after creating havoc in business, deflation brings down interest rates and prices for consumers, creating purchasing power. Once consumers are set to spend, the second part of the deflationary cycle is positive. That's what happened between 1982 and 1986.

Between 1990 and now—and I predict into 1997—we will be

seeing a second deflationary cycle. From 1990 to 1992 inflation started to recede again. The economy went into a recession, and businesses that couldn't compete began to fold. Although the situation of 1992 and into 1993 continues to worsen, according to my scenario, the deflation crisis bottoms out between late 1993 and 1994. Then the economy comes screaming out of the recession. Not only because the largest wave of baby boomers is set to buy houses and spend because of age demographics, but also because interest rates are going to be falling. Goods will be increasingly affordable with the continued progress of new technologies. Stronger, more efficient businesses will dominate the playing field, and therefore earn higher profits.

As we move into this deflationary time when new technologies are bringing down prices, spending habits of the new generation are lifting the economy. The two main growth areas for the 1990s and beyond will be long-term bonds and growth stocks. Especially look for stocks that are set to grow in this customized economy, those I identify in greater detail in Chapter 9.

The Spending Wave and other tools we discussed in earlier chapters tell us to look for three distinct periods: 1993 to 1997, 1998 to 2006, and 2006 on. So I have developed a set of strategies for each.

1993 to 1997

From 1993 into late 1997, we will see continued deflation, but more important, a rapid fall in interest rates. Economic growth will be dramatic. The huge government borrowing and general bankruptcy rates that drove up interest rates from 1992 to 1993 will begin to abate. Yet after prices fall in 1993, inflation will not return to any significant degree. We will see relatively stable prices after 1993 or 1994, even tending slightly toward continued deflation into 1997, with occasional mild bouts of inflation at the worst.

My best estimate is that interest rates will fall more moderately in 1994 and 1995 and then more dramatically from late 1996 into late 1997 or early 1998. But it's always hard to forecast interest rates accurately in the short term. Most investors should probably just buy and hold bonds from late 1993 to late 1997 or early 1998.

The greatest investment opportunity with the lowest risk in the next few years will come from buying long-term bonds. Get into 30-year Treasury bonds and long-term corporate bonds. Catch interest rates as they go up toward 10 percent or higher on 30-year Treasury bonds. Then ride the appreciation of those bonds as interest rates fall to 4 or 5 percent. Especially between 1994 and early 1998, I expect interest rates to literally plummet, so for the second half of 1993 on, I'm advising loading up on U.S. government bonds and quality corporate bonds. It means you will likely be able to double your money or better by early 1998.

U.S. Treasury bonds are a safe, government-backed investment giving a high yield while you're getting the appreciation.

This is our number one investment strategy for the early 1990s.

A brief explanation about long-term bonds. (If you already understand the mechanics of long-term bonds and the relationship between them and interest rates, skip ahead to the next section. If you don't understand bonds and want to learn more about them as investments, stick with me.)

You buy long-term bonds when interest rates are going to be high. A 30-year bond is guaranteed by the government to earn the interest rate in existence at the time you bought it—for 30 years.

To be safe, you can just sit there for 30 years and collect a 10 percent yield. Years down the road people may only be getting 4 or 5 percent on bonds. Many people in retirement or investors who want a high-yield fixed-income portfolio may want to ride out the term with bonds. They can let the bonds sit there and collect 10 percent.

For those who want nearer-term appreciation, the opportunity will be there with bonds. You see, bonds benefit from falling interest rates. So you want to load up on them at high rates and hope that interest rates fall later. Say you buy a bond for $10,000 that is guaranteed 10 percent interest on it for the entire 30 years the bond is outstanding. When rates fall to 5 percent, people are going to pay a huge premium to get 10 percent locked in for 30 years. The market will reflect that rate advantage by raising the value of your bond commensurate with the difference between the two rates over the life of the bond.

A typical 30-year government bond—if it goes from 10 percent to 5 percent—will approximately double in value. That bond you bought for $10,000 would be worth $20,000. For those who want to take higher risks and earn higher returns, you can buy zero-coupon Treasury bonds that are sold at huge discounts but pay no interest—the forgone interest is figured into the purchase price. Zero-coupon bonds could as much as quadruple instead of double under the same scenario—but realize that if you're wrong, your losses will double also.

I will talk about stocks in the next section. But even though stocks will also soar and probably double or better from late 1994 to 1997, bonds are typically considered to be a lower-risk investment. Even if I'm wrong, you have an investment that will pay you 10 percent or higher and is backed by the federal government. Therefore, bonds have a better risk-adjusted appreciation potential in this period.

So the number one investment to profit from in the coming turnaround in the economy is not stocks. But for the people who prefer investing in stocks or have companies that they know and favor, I suggest they accumulate stocks progressively between May and November of 1994—especially if you see the Dow Jones in the 1700 to 1800 area. But if you do this, you must have the conviction to hold such positions through the classic rockiness of such a bottoming process. Otherwise, I would concentrate more on the long-term government bonds or quality corporate bonds first and ride that from late 1993 into the time between 1994 and early 1998 when interest rates will fall most dramatically. Then start switching out of bonds.

> The ideal portfolio would switch into 60 to 80 percent long-term government or corporate bonds progressively in the second half of 1993 with 10 to 20 percent growth stocks and 5 to 10 percent money market funds or T-bills for liquidity.

1998 to 2006

From the beginning of 1998 to around 2006 to 2010, the greatest investment appreciation will take place in quality growth stocks. Stocks may be a bit conservative in the earlier stages of the new boom despite dramatic economic growth. Stocks are obviously going to be a bit shell-shocked after a series of crashes, especially in 1987 and 1993, despite the dramatic overall rise in stock prices from 1982 into 1992. So investors will naturally have an increased perception of risk and volatility in the market. But as the boom shows staying power, with little or no inflation and falling interest rates, stocks will take off. The greatest acceleration in stocks will occur precisely because interest rates move to such low yields by late 1997 or mid-1998. As we saw in 1987 and 1992, low interest rates not only signal economic growth to the stock market, but low rates motivate people holding bonds and money market funds to move into stocks for higher yields. My reading of the long-term indicators tells me that stocks will show the greatest relative appreciation versus other basic investments from early 1998 on.

> The forecasting tools show that stocks will conceivably climb to levels as high as 8500 between 2006 and 2010! The great majority of these gains should be made in two periods, between late 1994 to late 2000 or 2001 and then from 2002 to 2006 to 2010.

Bonds will continue to appreciate slowly, but they will have seen the majority of their gains between 1994 and 1998.

The second part of this recommendation is to buy the stocks that will grow in the coming boom. You'll have to read Chapters 9 and 10 to find the types of growth markets to expect and the types of business strategies that are going to work in the coming new economy. You should be able to look at any industry and gauge the potential of actual companies with the help of the models I project for success in the Customized Economy.

General stock recommendations   I'm not going to go down the list of the New York Stock Exchange and try to analyze and pick individual winners for you. In the first place, I couldn't presume to do it. Industry analysts in the brokerage houses spend their entire careers evaluating narrow segments of the broad market. However, I feel the best strategy is for you to rely on your personal knowledge and experience in your own business or industry or your particular consumer interests to identify stock and investment opportunities you can trust. I have met many people who bought stocks like Home Depot in the '80s and enjoyed handsome returns simply because they felt it was a great consumer concept that was bound to grow.

Use the quantitative and qualitative tools in this book to spot such opportunities. Then ask your broker to identify companies that meet your criteria. The broker can further scrutinize various risk and financial factors that affect companies you want to invest in. Here are some brief pointers. Look for stocks in companies with:

A customized bent. Look for the growth stocks—stocks that are going to grow with this Customized Economy. Remember the characteristics in Chapter 6? Look for these qualities in companies you want to invest in:

- Premium quality
- Customization

- Fast response and delivery
- Personalized service

International opportunities. Find companies that are set to benefit from the growth in the United States, Europe, Mexico, and Eastern Europe as discussed in the previous chapter. Be very selective in buying stocks in areas where Japan's crisis might have an adverse effect.

Leading-edge technologies. Every industry has its segment with aggressive R&D reputations and high-tech tendencies to stay on top of flexible software technologies. We'll be giving a complete description of these factors in Chapter 10.

Leading-edge management. Organizations that have evolved away from hierarchical, top-down structure and toward entrepreneurial, front-line decision making in direct response to customers will prosper in the new economy.

Strategic alliances. Small companies that ally themselves with larger ones to gain economies of scale and larger companies that joint-venture with smaller, innovation-oriented companies will be winners in the coming boom. Watch for larger companies with successful strategies for entering the new growth markets by spinning off smaller divisions to successfully compete in premium markets as Toyota did with Lexus.

The stock market scenario

Our tools allow us to make a best guess for the stock market to begin its boom possibly as early as mid-to-late 1993 but more likely from mid-to-late 1994 on. After an initial strong surge, we could see some smaller corrections from late 1996 into 1997. However, it will continue to be an upwardly moving market into 2000 or 2001. At the end of the year 2000 is when the baby boom housing spending momentum will start to top off. The market will continue strong, but that big surge is likely to end around late in 2000. Overall, from mid-1994 to late 2000 or 2001 is going to be the best time to be in the stock market.

> From late 1997 into mid-1998, I recommend shifting emphatically away from bonds, down to perhaps 10 to 20 percent of the portfolio, so you can move into the stock market to the tune of 70 to 80 percent stocks with 10 percent cash. The indicators say that from late 1997 or early 1998 on, stocks will show far greater appreciation than bonds until about 2000 or 2001.

From late 2000 into 2001, progressively lighten up on stocks and move into a strong cash position to await a potential significant correction in the market. Then in mid-to-late 2002, buy stocks again until the market nears its peak between 2006 and 2010. To be safe, progressively liquidate your portfolio out of stocks into short-term, safe government securities, like T-bills, between 2006 and 2010. Learn to identify the kind of company that will succeed in the Customized Economy by looking into Chapters 9, 10, and 11.

2006 on

Between 2006 and 2010, the chances of speculation and volatility increase as we begin to move toward what may become the greatest depression of all times. Therefore I recommend moving progressively into the safest of investment vehicles: 60 to 90 percent Treasury bills and 10 to 20 percent gold or other precious metals. The chances are stocks will continue up into 2010, but I suggest you not play those final years unless you know what you are doing.

Special areas of investment interest

Gold and silver   Gold is an inflation hedge, not a deflation hedge. When people realize we're moving into a period of deflation, gold will continue to lose its luster. In general, stay away from gold and silver in the 1990s. Those investments will behave more like commodities. In addition, countries with troubled economies like Russia and the Middle East will dump gold holdings to raise cash at the height of their economic crises. My indicators say gold should bottom out in 1994 and appreciate only slowly at best.

What will probably happen is that gold will spurt up in the early part of the crisis in early 1993—when the Japanese market crashes and things start looking uncertain globally—during the Tidal Wave from Tokyo. That's when the banking crisis will hit the world economy. But once the real deflation trends set in, gold will clearly become more of a commodity again, likely falling toward $200 an ounce. So if you must buy gold, wait until 1994, but don't expect a major bull market in gold. Only the sophisticated investor who understands gold should be a player taking advantage of short-term swings. Other people should avoid it.

Commodities   New technologies are going to keep materials and commodity prices down for most of the '90s and early 2000s. The technology wave is going to work against commodity prices. Oil is not going to be a good investment, so stay away from oil futures—especially in 1993.

Real estate   Now here's a mixed bag. Real estate should bottom in 1993 in many areas or, at the latest, 1994 in California and some other highly inflated areas. That means it will be a favorable time to buy real estate. As we boom, real estate will increase in value again, but it will behave more in accordance with the typical laws of supply and demand. It will not be as explosive in many areas as it was in the '70s and '80s, fueled by inflation.

Yes, real estate will go up if you buy good properties in a growing area. In most cases it will be a good investment from 1994 on, but the days of anybody buying just any house or any property and making tons of money are over. Although real estate will clearly benefit from the boom, it may not tend to appreciate as fast as growth stocks. Still, it is a leveraged investment that you can borrow against. And people will obviously still want to own their own homes and businesses will need to own strategic properties. For the real estate investor, I recommend three strategies:

Go for high quality in commercial properties. Once we get out of the recession, this will be a necessity. Businesses will feel obligated to upgrade their images in this boom as they move into high-quality custom markets. Since commercial real estate has been so overbuilt in many areas, there will be incredible bargains at the bottom of this recession.

Go for high quality in residential properties. Buy quality homes in quality areas. The largest number of baby boomers are going to be moving into their largest or main home in the buying surge between late 1993 and 2000. The homes that are going to sell for the biggest prices are the premium, larger homes. They will likewise tend to be hit the hardest in the recession, providing a great buying opportunity.

Go for the exurbs. The greatest growth areas in commercial and residential real estate are probably going to increasingly be the smaller towns and cities outside the huge congestion of metropolitan areas. In Chapter 9 we'll cover this in more detail, but we'll be seeing a new general trend in migration. We moved from the cities to the suburbs in the last technology cycle of the 1900s. In this cycle coming up, we'll see another migration to small towns and cities for safety, security, education, quality of life, and quality of environment. New technologies are going to allow people to work more at home or to relocate divisions of companies—software divisions, financial divisions—out in smaller towns and outer suburbs so people do not have to live in New York City or San Francisco or their bedroom communities.

> The best real estate appreciation is going to be in the emerging small towns and cities like Boise, Idaho, Madison, Wisconsin, and Provo, Utah—places like that. People will disperse to what they'll call the exurbs. That's the next great migration, which will occur over many decades as the new economy develops. So you don't want to be necessarily buying in downtown New York or San Francisco.

Investments that grow in the future are going to be real, tangible things, good companies, good bonds, and good real estate. We'll move away from inflation hedges and back into the investments that generate business growth. In the next chapter we'll take a closer look at how the Spending Wave and Innovation Wave of the baby boom generation will affect individual businesses and regional markets. Investors can pick particular stocks in their business specialties if they learn to watch those waves. Businesses will be able to use the waves to choose markets.

Now, as I've already suggested, you should examine any potential investment using the guides I'll introduce in the next three chapters.

9

Growth Markets
of the '90s

*What's hot and what's
not in the coming boom*

BULLETIN

You can identify the winning businesses in the coming
boom . . . *well before the boom even begins!* Think
of the implications of that. You can adapt your planning
and timetables to pinpoint new market segments before
they enter their most rapid growth periods. You can
use this recession as a time to prepare for the
unprecedented growth markets that will follow!

Don't get left behind in business

It's not enough to know about the existence of the coming boom,
even if it *is* the greatest boom in history. Sure, this boom will mean
a bigger pie with enormous prosperity. But it will also mean an
unbelievable intensification of competition for new growth markets.

The best time to gain an edge will be just as we come out of this recession. Many businesses will still be cautious or only marginally healthy. There will be a great opportunity to gain market share in your business. But you must be ready. You must analyze your markets, identify the winning segments, and be ready to move aggressively at the end of this recession.

That's what this chapter is about—how you can target the growth markets of the '90s in your business.

You must take control of your own destiny if you want to increase your odds of enjoying prosperity in the next 15 years or so. You must educate yourself about virgin products in new markets. You must track the progress of the newest niche products that are encroaching on established markets. You must judge when to enter the hot growth markets. You may choose to abandon not so hot products altogether—or you may want to adapt to the new Customized Economy, pumping new life into shrinking market segments.

Hot? Not so hot? How can you know which is which?

The first step is to put on new glasses! I tell people that I walk around looking at the world through a different pair of glasses. I see things from the point of view of the new Customized Economy and its principles of growth, productivity, and management. I see opportunities where others see decline. Why? Simply because they are looking at the old standardized businesses that are stagnating or decaying. I see the growth potential stemming from niche markets that are replacing those old standardized markets and products.

Most managers see only problems. They say, "Baby boomers don't follow orders, don't have the discipline needed to be productive in business."

I see baby boomers that are highly creative and productive. I know they can be highly motivated in the right environment. It's my conviction that we can grow if we change our management practices and organizational structure.

So I ask you to simply put on new glasses as well and open your eyes. Watch what's coming. The information is out there. All you have to do is learn to recognize it. I will give you the tools in this chapter to help you sharpen your eyesight. That way you can run ahead of the pack. You'll be able to recognize the trends as they occur and before they become visible to observers less astute than you. At a minimum you will avoid the pitfall of staying with products and market segments that guarantee certain failure.

We can take our two most basic tools, the Spending Wave and the Innovation Wave, and apply them to the prediction of individual markets and businesses, not just the macroeconomy. Let's look at the Spending Wave, because it tells us that baby boomers spend in predictable patterns. From the time they move into the work force, members of that generation gain experience, move up in their careers, become more productive, earn, and spend on a predictable timetable. They reach the peak in overall spending at about age 49. In fact, so many baby boomers simultaneously exhibit the same patterns of spending, we can predict the path of the economy.

Major categories of spending by industry

However obvious this may seem, I'm going to say it anyhow: baby boomers won't spend at the same age on every product. Figure 9-1 shows how spending peaks vary for broad categories of spending.

We can learn a lot about the general character of the coming boom by studying these consumer categories. Let's look at them briefly. I'll discuss each by describing its individual pattern and indicating its effect on the general boom.

Apparel. Spending for clothing peaks in the late 30s to early 40s. That's because younger adults are more fashion-conscious as they are climbing their career and social ladders and they have teenage kids who are very fashion-conscious.
Automobiles. Spending for transportation peaks in the late 40s, closely paralleling the overall spending peak.

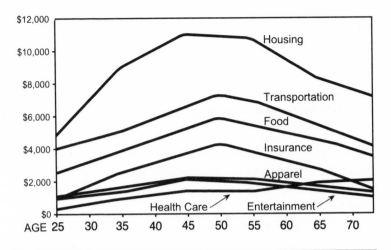

Figure 9-1. Spending patterns for various categories of major
industries
Source: U.S. Bureau of Labor Consumer Expenditures Survey,
Interview Survey, 1989

Entertainment. Spending for entertainment peaks in the late
30s or early 40s as younger adults spend more on entertainment—for themselves and their teenage kids.

Food. Food spending peaks in the late 40s along with the general
spending cycle, although food consumption at home peaks earlier. This is due to the influence of teenagers. As the kids start
to leave the nest, parents eat out more.

Health care. Costs for health care is the only basic category
that doesn't peak and decline. These costs just continue to climb
throughout a person's life. Then, in the last six months of life
or so, when the very largest percentage of health care costs
occur, these costs usually spike upward.

Insurance. Spending for insurance peaks in the late 40s and
early 50s, as most people have made the bulk of their plans to
provide for the family in case the head of the household dies.

And, of course, all-important to you and the industry is . . .

The special case of housing

Housing. As we've seen, the enormous impact of the largest generation in history making its largest investment on a predictable timetable sets the basic direction of our economy.

After the housing peak at age 43, spending on main homes drops off slowly into the ages of 48 to 49 and then the housing curve trails off dramatically. A minority of consumers will buy a second or vacation home in their 50s. Many will move into some type of retirement housing in the 60s and beyond.

Remember, baby boomers arrived in three waves. The first wave is about age 50. So they have already peaked in their spending overall and have been out of the main house market for a while. What will they be doing next? Buying vacation homes. The recession will cause a steep decline in vacation homes in many areas, particularly Hawaii. But it will be a good time to buy such homes as the first wave of baby boomers makes its foray into vacation homes with many years of second- and third-wave buying to follow. Builders should probably wait until the excess inventories are bought up and prices return upward substantially before entering the vacation home market.

The second wave of baby boomers turns 46 in 1993. They peaked in main home demand in 1990 but are still in their slowing plateau of home buying and will peak in their overall spending in late 1994. So they will not be a major factor in housing until they start buying vacation homes in the mid-to-late '90s.

While the extended recession is working off the overbuilt housing supply from the '80s, the huge third wave of baby boomers will be getting ready to drive the economy into the largest housing surge. The peak numbers of this wave will turn 32 to 36 this year. They will move in droves into the market for large main homes in the coming decade—from 1993 or 1994 to 2000 to 2004, to be more exact. I calculate that period by using our 43-year-old peak for house buying. In other words, housing will grow dramatically from

1993 to 2000 and then plateau into 2004 before the demand for main homes peaks. And don't forget, baby boomers will be moving to suburbs or more likely to exurbs, smaller towns and cities, when they can afford to be away from metropolitan areas. The greatest spending will occur in this market for residential main home real estate. For investors the high-end residential market will also tend to be the hardest hit in the recession, as the few people who do buy will go for lower-priced homes. However, after the recession this category will appreciate the most. Home builders will have to forget the starter houses that drove their growth in most areas in the past and get into the larger main homes. Remember, I have also forecast that interest rates will be in a strong down trend between 1994 and 1997, further encouraging people to buy larger homes with more options. You'll be able to buy close to double the house you can afford now, when mortgage rates come down, as I predict, to as low as 5 to 6 percent and real estate prices come down to reality during the recession. Again, this vastly increased purchasing power will more than offset any smaller declines in equity in starter homes. Therefore, the quality housing markets will clearly be where the growth is.

One of the greatest boom industries in the coming decade will be housing. But you just watch. Many home builders will misread the trends and go out and build those starter homes that few people will want. Yes, the starter home sold well in the past—at the time when baby boomers predictably wanted them! Sellers will have to discount starter homes to the smaller baby bust market before they learn the lesson of watching these spending trends. The people who understand age demographics and the Spending Wave will make larger main homes available. And they will have the housing consumers waiting on them in the areas they want to live in. It's all predictable.

The smart real estate firm will follow the curve from main homes toward vacation homes and toward retirement communities. They will profit from the baby boom generation in all of the phases of their life and housing cycles.

We will start to see apartments and multifamily rental housing begin to grow again in the mid-to-late '90s as the next generation's first wave begins to move into the labor force.

Every industry related to home building in general and luxury home building in particular—plumbing, cabinetry, lighting fixtures, carpet, tile, appliance, lumber, brick, window makers, pool manufacturers, recreation room equipment—should look toward making upgrades available for a growing upscale market in housing.

Narrowing the focus to individual products and services

In fact, age demographics permits us to refine patterns of spending even further than these broad categories. Every consumer product or service is age-driven and has its own age curve—from housing down to frankfurters and potato chips for products and veterinary care for services. Annual U.S. Bureau of Labor Consumer Statistics, Expenditures Surveys (Figure 9-2), give you access to spending habits in thousands of households. Here are three examples:

Potato chips peak around age 40. Now, you may ask, "Do people around age 40 really eat that many potato chips?" The answer is no. Teenage kids drive chip demand—statistics tell us that calorie intake peaks for the typical kid at age 14. It just so happens that the typical family has an average 14-year-old kid when the parents are around age 40. So potato chips peak. Many other junk foods and grocery items peak around this same time.
Veterinarian Services peak a little after age 40. You already know why, right? Yes, this is the age at which the children of those parents in the early 40s are most likely to have pets. Of course, when the kids leave, so do the pets.
Roofing repairs peak at a late age, around 68. Why would this be? Again, common sense gives us the answer. If most people

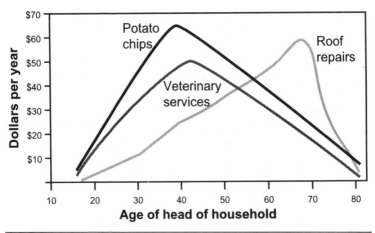

Figure 9-2. Average family spending by age for three products
and services
Source: U.S. Bureau of Labor Consumer Expenditures Survey, Interview and
Diary Survey, 1987

buy their main home in the early 40s, then many people are still
sitting in them in their late 60s. After 20 to 30 years the roof
needs repairing. Someone in their 60s is more likely than a 30-
year-old to say, "I'm not about to spend the weekend risking
my life to fix my roof or clean the gutters. I'll get Roto-Roofers
to come and do it."

Every consumer product or service has its own individual age-
driven Spending Wave, with most going up until some point in
life, peaking, and then declining predictably. In addition to health
care, which never reaches a peak, there are some categories
that break the mold. We saw in Chapter 2 how savings has two
successive peaks, one in the mid-40s for college and a higher
peak in the mid-70s for retirement. Well, there are some other
categories that follow this "double hump" pattern. One of them
is mattresses!

Why a "double hump" pattern in the spending curve for mattresses? Of course, the first peak in spending for mattresses
comes around age 43 when people buy that main home. Should
spending drop for good after the children leave the nest? You

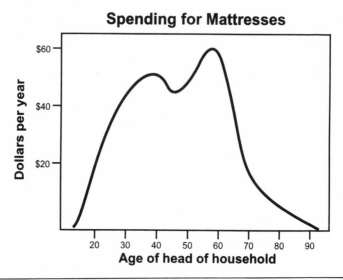

Figure 9-3. The average family spending curve, by age, for
mattresses
Source: U.S. Bureau of Labor Statistics, Consumer Expenditures Survey,
Interview and Diary Survey, 1987

would think so. Our statistics tell us otherwise. Just when the
kids leave, we arrive at the age when we get more frequent
pains in the back! So we buy new mattresses. Firmer, softer,
orthopedic, hospital—whatever the case, these mattresses will
be more expensive.

You can predict when individual consumer products and services will
grow, just as we predicted the track of the overall economy. Each
product will have its individual Spending Wave, allowing you to calculate when spending will peak for that product.

In general, we humans are predictable. If you open your eyes
to what is available, there lies in plain view a wealth of information

about when we, on average, buy diapers, clothing, housing, and pets, and when we have backaches and so on.

To get demographic information on the age-driven cycles of your consumers, see a booklet titled *Consumer Expenditures Surveys* at your local U.S. Government Printing Office bookstore. This booklet summarizes about sixty major categories of spending.

A computer service I have developed gives me year-by-year Spending Waves for any of hundreds of detailed categories in the survey. For information on that service, see the back of this book.

Ultimately, the best way for your consumer-oriented business to target age demographics is to start collecting age and other demographic data on your customers. I recommend that most businesses develop their own customized Spending Wave curves for each distinct market of customers they serve. They can then use the local or regional statistics on the population distribution by age to project future spending and growth in your markets.

You can project an individual product's or service's Spending Wave into any country, state, county, zip code, or even neighborhood. We can project spending on an individual product in any local market or region by knowing two things. First is the Spending Wave for the product. Second is the age distribution for the market or region. Once you obtain local statistics on the population distribution by age, you can project how their spending on a product will predictably change as they age.

For example, you already know the pattern for potato chip consumption by age. In any zip code zone in the nation where you can determine that there is a large population of teenagers approaching the 14-year-old-peak, you can locate the best growth markets for potato chips and project, at least in rough terms, what spending will be for chips. Our economy is far more predictable, even at the microlevel, than we have ever assumed.

I have constructed a model that manipulates the endless maze of details of products and local markets. It allows me to give quick, low-cost data to businesses and individuals interested in forecasting everything from when and where they should buy a home to where in local markets individual products will be growing. I used that model to give you an insight into the top-20 consumer product categories for growth in consumer spending in the next decade. Here's . . .

What's hot

This list, compiled from my demographic computer model, of the top-20 growth areas in percentage terms shows what to look for from 1994 to 2004 during the great boom. This list is arranged with the hottest on top.

A Top-20 List of Products and Services
- Motorized camper coaches
- Motorboats
- Roof and gutter maintenance
- College tuition
- Men's sport coats
- Refrigerators/freezers purchased and installed
- Stoves, ovens
- Domestic service
- Auto rental
- School books and supplies for college
- Men's sweaters and vests
- Women's dresses
- Winter sports equipment
- Wall-to-wall carpet installation
- Elementary school and high school tuition
- Women's accessories
- Club membership dues and fees
- Accounting fees
- Men's coats and jackets
- Eyeglasses and contact lenses

A rule of thumb: The largest markets of the '90s will be dominated by the purchases of baby boomers moving into the 35-to-44 age range and their one- to 10-year-old children. Those are the two largest growth segments stemming from age demographics. But the highest percentage of growth will come from products that peak in the 45-to-54 age range as the baby boomers of the leading edge enter this age category. You can peruse *Consumer Expenditures Surveys* and see which products peak in these age ranges. Also examine the quality issue. As they age and earn higher incomes, baby boomers will upgrade into quality in most purchases. This means large suburban homes, high-quality cars, station wagons and minivans, golf as a sport, and so on. Here are some of the general categories in addition to the more specific ones we have listed above. You could expect growth in these in the coming decade as baby boomers move into the 35-to-44 age range:

- Home computers and software
- Most foods (remember those 14-year-olds)
- Restaurants—family-style for when the kids get to go out and upscale when it's parents' night only
- Upgrade automobiles
- Larger family houses
- Furniture and appliances
- Life insurance
- Checking and savings deposits
- Mortgage lending
- Investment brokerage
- Children's and adult clothing
- Entertainment
- Medical and dental services
- Business travel
- Commercial construction

What's *not* hot?

Here, arranged with the area of least growth at the top of the list,
are the Bottom-20 products and services. You'll notice that many
of these are related to younger children's needs and interests.
That's for the obvious reason that during this boom period children
of baby boomers will be transitioning into adolescence and young
adulthood.

A Bottom-20 List of Products and Services
- Babysitting
- Day-care and preschool expenses
- Infant undergarments
- Bicycles
- Video game hardware and software
- Care in convalescent or nursing homes
- Coin-operated laundry and dry cleaning services
- Used trucks
- Toys, games, hobbies, and tricycles
- Girls' skirts and pants
- Girls' shirts, blouses, and sweaters
- Boys' pants
- Rental videocassettes
- Photographic equipment
- Fees for recreational lessons
- Reupholstery of furniture
- Videocassettes, tapes, and discs
- Pet supplies and medicine
- Kitchen and dining room furniture
- Telephones and accessories

Technological and social S-Curves of the baby boom generation

The common denominators of the new products and services that are moving into our economy are not necessarily distinctions between high tech and low tech but four basic qualities that baby boomers bring to the marketplace. We discussed these in some detail in Chapter 5. Call them preferences or demands, whatever you please. Like it or not, baby boomers demand:

- High-quality, value-added products and services
- Customization to individual needs
- Fast response and quick delivery
- Personalized service

These four preferences are the most fundamental factors driving what I have called the Customized Economy. When a group the size of the baby boom generation exhibits clear preferences, the sheer numbers create a demand in the marketplace. Learn to recognize it, and plot your strategies on how to capitalize on it.

From niche markets to the mainstream in the coming boom

While your attention has been diverted by the inflation of the '70s and the economic smoke screens of the '80s, a tremendous period of technological innovation has been taking place. All kinds of new products and services have been developed. Despite the tendency to believe that those new technologies will remain as niche markets, they have been gaining increasing market share from older, standardized products. Many of them, developed by entrepreneurs from the baby boom generation and many others who recognize the potential of baby boomer demand, are poised to take off on the growth phase as they are adopted into the mainstream economy.

The trick is to identify products moving from niche market positions, say, of 10 to 50 percent toward 50 to 90 percent in the coming boom years. These will occur in virtually every industry.

Examples of past S-Curves I've already examined the acceptance of radial versus bias-ply tires and the adoption of automobiles until the average family owns two cars. Other examples from the past include:

- CDs replace records in '80s
- ATM machines in walk-up locations in '70s and early '80s
- Credit cards—'60s and '70s and '80s
- Desktop microcomputers in the office or office automation in late '70s through '80s

Examples of emerging S-Curves for the '90s

- Luxury cars—10 percent in late '80s, moving toward 90 percent around 2010.
- Dual-traction tires for all-weather driving
- Fax machines
- Cellular phones in cars
- Sales force/front-line automation with laptop/notebook computers—less than 5 percent now, moving toward 10 percent in the mid-'90s and around 90 percent by the top of the boom.
- Environmental cleanup industries—these hit the 10 percent springboard around the late 1980s. Their growth and numbers will mushroom toward 90 percent by the end of the boom—leading to massive legislation and business opportunities in "cleanup."
- Higher-quality, fresh, ethnic and specialty fast food—from Colombo's frozen yogurt to Il Fornaio Italian bakeries in San Francisco to Häagen-Dazs and Gelato Classico ice cream shops to La Petite Boulangerie to California Pizza Kitchen

- Upscale Italian men's fashions—flowery, bright ties; pleated pants, no back vents, cuffed pants, and oversized cuts
- Flexible production machinery versus standardized machines
- Bed & breakfast hotels and concierge floors of hotels
- Specialty chemicals
- Specialty steels
- Mini-mills in regional markets
- Custom semiconductor chips
- Hi-tech plastic bathroom stalls
- White-collar pool halls
- Drive-up ATM machines now replacing walk-up ATMs
- Boutique specialty chain stores—from clothes to delis
- Home delivery of groceries and other foods and products
- Super-premium foods—Ben & Jerry's, Häagen-Dazs ice cream
- Premium garden tools—Smith & Hawken

The next chapter will examine a selection of these products and services in greater detail to show how business strategies will be changing in the next decades.

What emerging S-Curves are approaching 10 to 90 percent?

Six clues to identifying S-Curves about to take off
- Is this a steady trend over time or is it more faddish?
- Would this product or service be used by broader markets if the price came down or it became substantially easier to use or learn?
- Has the product achieved a strong niche position accounting for 5 to 10 percent of its potential market?
- In consumer markets, has this product or service already successfully penetrated the upper-income or young urban professional markets and is now just starting to attract upper-middle-class buyers?
- Has the product or service shown steady downward cost and price progress, thereby attracting broader markets?
- Is the product or service in sync with the four basic qualities

of the Customized Economy or with key social trends that we
will discuss in the last section of this chapter?

Looking for the second wave of most S-Curve trends   As
we saw in Chapter 6, most trends require two S-Curves of innovation and growth to complete themselves. The first S-Curve
establishes a radical innovation or a new direction. The second S-
Curve appears toward the maturity or 90 percent phase of the
first. It brings incremental innovations and directions that extend
the trend and shove it into the mainstream. These two trends
together proceed in the four-stage product life cycle sequence of
innovation, growth, boom, shakeout, and maturity boom.

Every business should examine emerging new segments in its
marketplace. Look for trends forming along the lines of the new
Customized Economy. Look for signs of the maturing of a first
phase and the emergence of a follow-on phase. Since such an
emergence should be occurring during a shakeout phase in the
product or industry, don't be distracted by the turbulence of that
shakeout.

I gave an example in Chapter 5 of notebook computers forming
a second S-Curve of growth during the shakeout of desktop PCs.

You can find examples in your own industry. Just look for this
two-step innovation and growth phase of S-Curves. Examine past
growth segments that appear to be slowing or maturing—approaching their 90 to 100 percent phase on the S-Curve. Look for
the incremental innovations that are creating the next S-Curve.
Remember, you can track that new S-Curve's growth if you can
find the 10 percent takeoff point of market penetration. You'll find
this second S-Curve in its entrepreneurial or innovation phase while
the old S-Curve is maturing in a shakeout period. If you understand
the S-Curve and product life cycle principles you will almost always
see growth and opportunity where others see maturity and limi-
tation.

Here are two brief examples:

Diffusion fashions   In the fashion industry we saw a very
clear, radical S-Curve appear in the '70s—designer clothing. For

a price you could get a designer's name on clothing that projected an image and propped up the ego. So we had all of the classic signs of a new S-Curve emerging: premium price, steady growth over time, a clear niche market. But in the late '80s the higher-income markets became saturated and growth slowed. We started to see some shakeout in that industry.

But lately we have also seen a clear new S-Curve emerging. The new lines of clothing are called diffusion fashions. Figure 9-4 shows the relationship between the two curves.

Designers are taking their high-end fashion designs and bringing them down into affordability by using less expensive fabrics and cutting the extra tailoring. This is creating a new growth market aiming at upper-middle-class or early adopters. Expect diffusion fashions to mushroom in the second phase of this boom to an even greater extent than did the designer lines of the '70s and '80s.

Automatic teller machines
In the early '70s, young, urban, affluent baby boomers started using walk-up automated teller ma-

S-Curves for Fashions

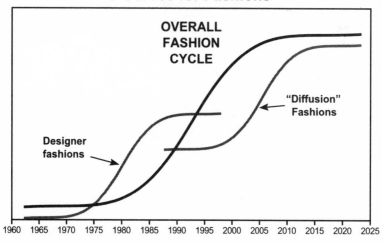

Figure 9-4. Overlapping S-Curves of designer and "diffusion" fashions

chines at their banks. ATMs went into their 10 to 90 percent growth stage in the late '70s and early '80s. Consumers found them more convenient than going into the bank. Besides, at the end of the month, it's a heck of a lot less embarrassing to draw $5 in cash via a machine that doesn't smirk at you than it is to write a check for a carton of milk.

What happened in the early to mid-'80s as walk-up machines were beginning to mature? As S-Curve dynamics would have predicted, we saw a new S-Curve emerge—drive-up ATMs.

Drive-up ATM machines are approaching the 10 percent takeoff point into their growth stage in 1993. So we can see—better than most of the experts—that this is the threshold to the next stage of rapid growth. Many industry professionals write off drive-up ATMs as a maturing niche market with little growth potential.

Do you want to bet on the experts here? Or do you want to bet on the S-Curve?

History would say, "Take the S-Curve." I've read the consumer surveys. They clearly show that much broader segments of the

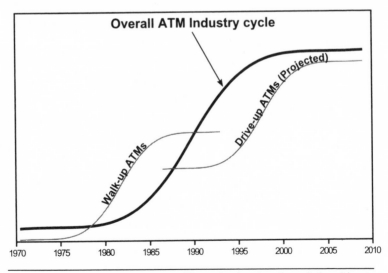

Figure 9-5. The ATM industry life cycle showing the relationship between walk-ups and drive-ups

population are interested in drive-up ATM machines. When drive-up machines are available at the same location as walk-ups, the drive-ups will get anywhere from 20 to 100 percent more use. People use them when they are available. That's what counts!

The smartest banks are finding, as all bias-ply tire manufacturers eventually realized about radials, that the new kid on the block is much more than a niche market. Drive-ups attract the best customers and have higher volumes of use than walk-ups. So they are more profitable than walk-ups. Inevitably, they will come down in cost. The S-Curve and cost dynamics tell us that we're on the verge of a growth explosion in drive-up ATMs. For the smart investors and astute businesses there is a clear investment opportunity here.

As I've said, the S-Curve applies not only to products and services but to social and other trends. So let's look at some of the leading social trends that will be shaping consumer behavior and product development in the '90s.

Qualitative social S-Curve trends

Environmental concern. We can't grow without taking the environment into account. As a concern, it will grow in consumers' minds to become a top priority. The environment will become a huge industry. From recycling to pollution control equipment to consciousness products like fake furs and nonfluorocarbon sprays, look for growth. This trend clearly moved into its takeoff phase in the late '80s and will continue to grow straight uphill during the boom. Voters will demand more and more legislation to protect the environment. Businesses will find ways to minimize their environmental impact. Smart businesses will profit from the trend.

For example, oil companies will be seeing declining demand and falling prices for oil anyhow. Why shouldn't they see themselves as uniquely qualified to enter the environmental cleanup and restoration businesses? In the past, oil has been the number one polluting industry in the world. Arguably, this was not the oil industry's creation, but consumer demand for petroleum products. Times have changed, though. Now the environment has become a major concern—therefore an opportunity. The oil companies have experience in cleanup, experience obtained by "accident." Since the environmental cleanup business is similar to exploration—that is, it requires geological skills, high capital expenditures, and precision risk analysis—I think environmental cleanup will grow far more as an industry than solar energy.

Education. The new Conformist civic-minded generation being born in the '80s and 90s will be the best educated in history because of the concerns of their baby boomer parents. Generally everybody agrees on the failure of the present system. As defense spending wanes, education will become the key concern of voters. Education will surely evolve toward more choice and local control and input. Products and services from industries with education will prosper. Alternative education programs and private programs will be increasingly blended into the public schools in a variety of ways.

Great migration to the "exurbs" or small towns and cities. We moved to the suburbs after the last great economic revolution. This time we will move to smaller towns and cities for safety, environmental quality, better education, and more intimate neighborhoods. This will cause infrastructure and tax problems in the larger cities and some suburban areas. Hundreds of boom towns will experience growth and growing pains. This trend will greatly affect everything from housing and commercial construction to political power to retail stores.

Health care reform. The consumer as patient is getting smarter. This is an S-Curve that is clearly at or near its takeoff point. Two fundamental reasons have caused runaway health care costs: First is the high-cost, high-tech machinery and methods for keeping people alive in the last months of life. In other words, we have again applied new technologies to first preserving the old system of "Cure it after it happens and at all costs."

Second is unnecessary procedures—operations and costly solutions from miracle pills to removal of organs.

Preventive care and alternative health care practices will grow—from acupuncture to physical therapy to sports medicine to food and vitamin therapy. We may even see National Health Care as a last desperate attempt to lower the high cost of health care.

In general, we will see more choice and more patients taking responsibility for their own health. Doctors and other health care practitioners will more often become consultants to patients, helping them to understand their alternatives and their bodies and immune systems so they can choose the proper care wisely. Most important, we will see people learn to prevent disease and ill health rather than focusing on curing diseases after symptoms appear.

As preventive and alternative health practices move into the mainstream, we will see insurance policies and Health Maintenance Organizations (HMOs) and Preferred Provider Organizations (PPOs) increasingly cover these practices. We will also see more traditional and alternative health practitioners allying themselves together in practices and institutions that offer the best of both worlds. We have already seen and will see more products and services that are self-diagnostic and are offered outpatient style nearer to or in the home or office.

Moving the work to the worker. It must be obvious in light of the huge environmental threats and concerns we have today that we simply have to change the nature of work and the endless cycle of longer and longer commuting. Add to this the increasing time constraints on the two-worker family. We must and we will recognize that we can use new technologies to move work to the worker and cut out unnecessary commuting. This will happen in many ways:

- Moving entire departments into neighborhood offices near where people want to live—in the suburbs and exurbs. This saves the company overhead and saves the workers time and commuting costs.

- Allowing more individual workers, especially sales and service, entrepreneurial, and mobile technical, maintenance, and professionals to work out of their homes.
- Relocating larger offices to lower-cost, more worker-convenient small-town and suburban locations.
- Offering more consulting, management, communications, and sales services via telecommunications that allow visual contact and interaction without travel.

Of course, travel and commuting will still be required where necessary for truly personal interaction and the human touch. This means that we will be designing more products so that we can minimize inventory and hard goods movement by customizing those products with computer software or chips or by adding the last steps of production at the retail store—the front line. Wherever possible, we will move people less in cars and airplanes.

As a speaker who travels weekly, I am looking forward to the day when it will be economical to use fully interactive video communications. Then I can speak to or consult with a group from my home office with the ability to answer questions and interact fully.

This trend ultimately means that our trucking and airline and automotive and energy businesses will start peaking in their growth at some point, even despite the huge growth trends of this boom. We simply must restrict movement of goods and people, and, of course, do it in ways that increase the goods and services and lifestyles for consumers. This will happen.

The women's movement moves on   We'll see greater

strides in the opportunities and contributions for women in the coming decades. We will see a second stage of the women's movement that will be far more effective in catapulting women into full participation at all levels of work and life.

In fact, this is a great example of how any new S-Curve trend takes two innovations and growth phases to complete an entire cycle. We can picture the women's movement as in Figure 9-6.

The first S-Curve of the women's movement was to confront

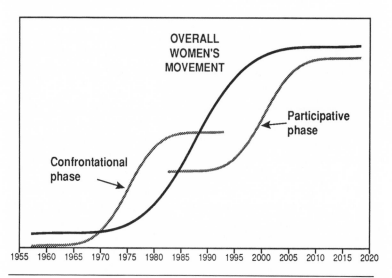

Figure 9-6. S-Curves of the women's movement

our male-dominated society, including legal and social systems. Women had to be on the attack to break down barriers to promotion, pay, access, and so on. And, of course, many of those barriers still exist.

Women have made great strides in raising the consciousness of society. They have gone through the personal struggles and soul-searching over issues like competing with men in the workplace and splitting home and career duties. They are more clear about their lives and their roles in society. Many women now want to feel the freedom to choose to stay at home. Many more want to continue to pursue challenging and lucrative careers in the workplace without competition, confrontation, and sexual abuse.

A new wave is already emerging with a whole new host of best-selling books and ideas. The triumvirate of the William Kennedy Smith trial, Clarence Thomas's confirmation hearing, and the announcement that Magic Johnson has the AIDS virus had a great and irrevocable impact on men's sensitivity to women's and sexual issues. Now that men are more aware of their effect on women in the workplace, they are increasingly open to dealing with these basic issues. I sense that we will see the women's movement take a new turn. It will move from anti-male toward a more confident pro-women stance.

Baby-boom managers will have less resistance to the integration of women and minorities into the work force.

Even more important will be the new managerial skills required in the corporation of the future. Supervisors are going to require a much greater degree of coaching and support of workers. This new style of management and business, if anything, clearly favors women and their natural approach to things and will become one of our country's key competitive edges in the coming customized economy.

The ultimate melting pot

We've seen the greatest civil rights movement struggle in this country of any in the world. The May 1992 riots in Los Angeles demonstrate how we have further to go on this difficult issue. However, there is a way to view the amelioration of racial strife as another investment that will pay huge dividends in our increasingly global, Customized Economy.

As with the women's movement, we are likely to see a second phase in the civil rights movement. Minorities will begin to capitalize on their strengths, skills, and contributions by communicating them aggressively. Meanwhile, the rest of society must learn to embrace the resources of diverse, fiercely independent cultures. Such diversity will give us an advantage over more homogeneous cultures like Germany and Japan in attacking diverse markets in the global economy.

Retail restructuring

Faith Popcorn, in her book *The Popcorn Report* (Doubleday Currency, 1991), identifies three types of retailing trends we can expect to see in the future. I agree with her on the following themes:

Home delivery. Many basic products and services will move toward home via quick delivery—you might even have a standing order that is delivered to your home on schedule the way milk and bread were once delivered. What firms like Federal Express and UPS have done for the letter and package delivery industry will be redone for a different segment of home delivery. Look for home delivery specialists working for many of your local businesses as well as improved responsiveness in catalogue shopping. The larger retailers will develop their own capacities for same-day delivery. Don't be surprised if your grocery store moves into the new age of economics by dropping back into providing a service from yesteryear—home delivery of groceries. We already see a trend back to the old-fashioned milkman. And why not clothing, sundries, books, and other department store products? For many of us, getting quick delivery—and virtually *NOW!*—is the highest priority.

Local specialized merchants. These businesses will deliver a high degree of personalized and customized service where necessary—specialty clothes, business services, specialty restaurants, neighborhood bars, catering services, and so on. In other words, everywhere that we truly need and require personalized service, those products and services will be dominated by small local enterprises where possible. Stores and services that can deliver the personal touch will make life more worthwhile for most of us. Therefore, we will continue to see new S-Curves emerging and growing in a wide variety of specialty products, mail-order catalogue companies, local services, and national chains. This is where small is clearly beautiful.

Large, interactive retailers. These stores will demonstrate products and provide some level of entertainment to help sell. A good example is in sports and exercise equipment. You've probably already seen television footage of ski shops with automated roller belt ski slopes in artificial alpine settings so customers can try out the equipment and clothing in action (or just show off for other shoppers). Here's a case where big is beautiful. Many small stores cannot afford the equipment to demonstrate or a wide enough inventory for demonstration and instant delivery that a large store can.

This is where malls will begin to evolve—toward large stores that can effectively demonstrate products that are not basic staples. They will provide a means for consumers to make better buying evaluations of more complex or higher-priced goods and services, while providing family entertainment. Families will want both in the little time they have outside of work and commuting.

Bottom line?

The trick in any business, especially any consumer business, is to follow that baby boom bulge. Every time they age another five years their psychological, social, and buying habits change dramatically. We've already seen the peak of the BMW-Rolex status trend because baby boomers have begun concentrating on their families and more practical things. They are no longer trying to impress their bosses and colleagues with status-oriented material possessions as they did in the early stages of their careers. Businesses must target markets that will grow directly or indirectly with the needs of 35- to 45-year-olds and their one- to 10-year-old children as they grow up.

If you seriously analyze age demographics, S-Curve patterns of growth, and the basic qualitative trends being generated by the inner-directed revolution of baby boomers, you will rarely miss the growth markets of the '90s.

Those qualitative trends will affect in fundamental ways the shape of the economy to come. So important are they that I have devoted the next chapter to telling you how you should adapt your business strategy to those trends for the coming new economy.

10

Business Strategies for the '90s

The fierce battle for
mainstream markets

BULLETIN

Stand by for good news and bad news. First, the good news: The new economy will provide enough growth markets for both emerging and mature companies that can appeal to the growing quality and customized segments of the marketplace. The bad news? Small and large companies will find themselves in a heated battle for these markets as they move into the mainstream.

The three basic market segments
in all industries

Every industry can be segmented into three basic divisions: a premium-quality segment, a value/discount segment, and a standard-quality segment. I have defined these segments according to a useful color code—blue-chip, red-chip, and yellow-chip. If it helps, think of poker chips. Highest in value are usually the blue chips. Red chips are second in value to blue. Think of yellow as white chips that have yellowed, as having a declining value.

Blue-chip. A common term to denote high quality is blue-chip. That idea holds up here. The blue-chip is the premium sector of an industry, specializing in high quality, customization, and personalized service with fast response and quick delivery. Chances are good that these companies have grown up relatively recently in an entrepreneurial environment with innovative management and fresh approaches to their customers. In retailing, you would call Nordstrom a blue-chip company. On anybody's list of blue-chip car companies you would find BMW, and more recently Lexus. The future in the coming boom will belong to the companies that fit my definition of blue-chip. The most success will fall to the blue-chip companies that can bring their quality into mainstream affordability.

Red-chip. Think of red-chip companies as hot in the past, but only warm in the future. This is the value/discount segment. These companies have made substantial incremental improvements over standard-quality yellow firms, bringing high value into their industries with discount prices, often accompanied by improved quality and service to boot. Naturally, they have taken market share from the yellow companies. You'd call Wal-Mart a red-chip company in retailing. Toyota is an excellent example of a red automobile company. These companies have been hot in the '80s for their ability to revitalize in the maturing, standardized, yellow industries. In the '90s they will have to adapt to the inner-directed generation or they'll ultimately slow in their growth in countries like the United States. There will also be opportunities to move their operations overseas to countries that are industrializing and therefore embracing the Standardized Economy.

Yellow-chip. This is the old standard-quality, mass-market sector in the economy. Think of aging when you think of a yellow company. These shrinking companies in mature industries grew up in the assembly-line Standardized Economy. You would probably find hierarchical management structures and a tendency toward bureaucracy. As we discussed in Chapter 4, these companies are losing ground in the new, Customized Economy. In retailing, you would call Sears a yellow company. In automobiles, you'd have to pick any of the Big Three. The past belongs to yellow companies—only the ones that can switch to red strategies will be able to survive in the future.

After only a moment's reflection, you could identify the blue, yellow, and red segments of our better-known industries. Of course, you could even further segment within each of these. For example, within the blue-chip segment of the car industry, we see different consumers looking for different qualities. When I say Mercedes, Continental, Cadillac, Porsche, BMW, Volvo, Acura, Lexus or Infiniti you get different mental images of personalities of buyers. (I think one of the best ways of segmenting consumers by lifestyle is in the type of car they buy. A car purchase and clothing buys are probably the clearest lifestyle statement consumers make.) Even within Mercedes you find a range of choices from the more practical 190 class, to the large luxury sedan class, to the sexy 500 SL sports car. But for now, let's not make distinctions too fine. Just understand these blue, red, and yellow segments to be characteristic of all industries. It's up to you to identify segments within the larger cuts. Many of the people I've taught my system to now use it as part of their permanent business vocabulary because it is so descriptive.

Over time, you've witnessed the changing relationship between these three segments, perhaps without even realizing it. Just to keep you thinking on the right track, here are some examples, with some companies listed by name and others by business segments.

Both the red and blue growth segments represent the beginnings of an ultimate restructuring of the yellow component in every industry—a restructuring that will create new winners and losers over the coming decade. This restructuring will look like Figure 10-2.

Blue (Premium)	Yellow (Standard)	Red (Value/Discount)
Nordstrom	Sears	Wal-Mart, K-Mart
Lexus, BMW	GM, Ford, Chrysler	Toyota, Nissan
Local financial planners	Merrill Lynch	Charles Schwab
Sammy's Wood-Fired Pizza–La Jolla	Pizza Hut	Dominos
Giorgio Armani, Donna Karan	Arrow, Jantzen	Levis, L.L. Bean
Bed & breakfast hotels Westin, Marriott	Holiday Inn, Ramada, Best Western	Hampton Inn, Motel 6, Red Roof Inn
Cypress Semiconductor	Intel, Motorola	NEC, Toshiba, Fujitsu
Jordan, Montelena	Almaden, Taylor	Gallo, Glen Ellen
Federal Express, UPS next day	U.S. Postal Service	UPS
Midwest Express, Alaskan	Continental, TWA	American, United, Delta

Figure 10-1. Table showing examples of blue-chip, yellow-chip, and red-chip segments found in any industry

As you can see, the yellow, standardized segment will be pinched out altogether by the turn of the century in most markets. This doesn't mean that all those businesses are doomed to die. But it does mean they will have to restructure in relation to the other segments or they'll have to reorganize. The red, value/discount segment has accounted for the greatest overall growth in the past—but the blue-chip, premium businesses will come on the strongest in the future, following a predictable S-Curve path in growth as the cost of quality comes down rapidly. Blue-chip segments will begin to dominate most industries by the end of the

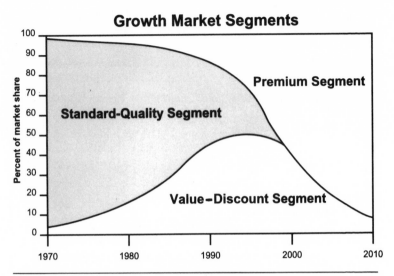

Figure 10-2. The future of the three segments in any
marketplace

coming boom. This means, in effect, that they will become the
next yellow, or standard-quality, segment as the upscale quality of
today becomes the standard of tomorrow. As we've said before,
this has always happened throughout history.

Premium needn't mean high-tech

Most mature businesses see the red segment in their industries.
But many question if there are really blue-chip segments emerging.
However, I haven't seen one industry in which a clear-cut blue-
chip segment wasn't at least emerging. Here are two examples of
premium segments being established in the most unlikely of old,
mature marketplaces:

Bathroom stalls. I read about a company that sells stalls made
from high-tech plastics that have the dual advantages of being

better-looking and graffiti-proof. High-end hotels and other up-scale establishments are paying two to three times more for these stalls in order to enhance their premium image. Do you think the old painted metal stalls will last as these high-tech stalls come down in price? No way.

Upscale pool halls. One company is growing as fast as it can spawn new franchises in the new market for white-collar pool halls. As we move increasingly from a blue-collar to a white-collar society, many people still like to go out and socialize over a game of pool. But they don't want to go to smoke-filled rooms with peanut shells and beer cans on the floor. It doesn't fit their image. So this company provides a clean, classy atmosphere and concentrates on personalized service.

What do all of these growing, premium segments have in common?

High quality, greater choice and customization, faster response and delivery, and personalized service, the characteristics of the Customized Economy.

The inner-directed revolution reviewed

The characteristics of the inner-directed generation are critical to understanding the dynamics of the blue-chip revolution.

From the outer-directed generation of Bob Hope and Ronald Reagan, we heard, "How can I adapt to the system and improve upon it by working from within. How can I be part of the team and help move forward with our _____ (fill in the blank here with *company, country, church, society, school board, political party,* and so on)?"

From the inner perspective, baby boomers are more likely to say, "Wait a minute. What do I want to do? What am I best at? Where am I most productive? What type of lifestyle would I prefer? How can I reshape institutions to achieve what I want?" These members of the radical innovator generation prefer not to adapt to the old Conformist ways of doing things. Instead, they will reshape the system to fit their values—the entrepreneurial approach.

That is a simple but significant change in perspective. Otherwise, people are the same. They still want houses, cars, money, happiness, privacy, kids (albeit fewer of them), and clean, healthy lifestyles and environments. But their differing perspective and the enormous power of sheer numbers will drive change as the baby-boom generation moves into its peak spending years in the economy and into positions of power in organizations.

Inner-directed trends   Here are some of the broad, inner-directed trends that will be taking us from an economy of mass markets to one of many highly segmented markets. Expect trends to be moving from . . .

Cost to quality in goods and services. Baby boomers value high quality and are willing to pay for it when it's important to them.

Hard sell to soft sell. You can't cram it down the throat of an inner-directed person. You have to help them make the right buying decisions by giving pertinent information—and let them feel that they've made the decision.

Buyer beware to seller beware. The inner-directed person isn't likely to accept poor-quality products and services or be treated impersonally. They expect businesses and producers to take their needs, from safety to reliability, into account. They expect businesses to communicate honestly with them. If they think they've been misled or victimized by negligence, they're going to demand corrective action—and they'll probably get it from their court system.

Conformity to individuality. This trend will become apparent in the work force as well as in the traits of the customer base. Organizations that foster the spirit of entrepreneurialism and innovation will benefit most from this trend. Companies that give their customers caring personal touches will enjoy profitable rewards.

Management-directed toward participatory management.
The new breed of employees is much more likely to insist on
being involved in decisions that affect them.
Centralization in organization toward decentralization.
Less bureaucracy will be a must in trying to suit individual requirements of consumers. If every customer becomes a market,
then every employee will become an entrepreneur or a business
unit.
Work ethic toward a leisure ethic. When I say this, people
take it to mean that this country is going down the tubes. Not
so. The leisure ethic doesn't say people are lazy. What it says
is that people will be most motivated when their work is creative,
challenging, and enjoyable, not rote and systematic.
Material satisfaction toward experiential satisfaction.
Inner-directed consumers are looking to experience and to
learn—to get more than just material satisfaction from products
and services. Employees are looking for self-esteem and satisfaction in their work.

This summary list of trends should be warning you that we're
in for a major shift—what used to work won't work any longer.
Such a shift in perspective demands more than an incremental
improvement in efforts to meet expectations. It demands a leap
in delivery of products and services, if not an absolute reversal
of customary trends.

What matters is that there are so many members of this generation
that they have the buying power to influence the outcome in the
competitive battles of the future. Baby boomers are also going to be
increasingly in the power positions of business and politics.

The companies that are establishing new niches are almost always emphasizing one or more characteristics of baby boomers to
differentiate themselves and to command premium prices. Therefore, any consistent growth segment that is emphasizing these

characteristics is likely to be around for the long term and is not a short-term fad or a limited niche market.

For me, the bottom line is this: We have experienced a quiet entrepreneurial revolution in the '70s and '80s, but that revolution is about to break out noisily, accelerating in growth as our economy screams out of its recession. Soon it will be apparent to all but the most reluctant economic observers that a blue-chip, premium economy is forming on top of our red, value/discount economy, even as it takes over from the yellow, standardized economy. That premium economy is primarily based on customization. We are moving from a time of standardized products to one where they are being replaced wherever possible by customized, high-value products and services. This movement started as mass markets matured in the '60s, moved to segmented markets in the '70s, and settled into niche marketing in the '80s.

So what is it going to be called in the '90s? Individualized marketing. Every customer will become a market. And how will that be done? Through one of America's greatest strengths, an area where we lead the world—in flexible customizing software.

Every customer a market—using software to customize

The social trends I discussed earlier are such that consumers are already beginning to demand quality, customization, fast response, and personalized service. These demands are being passed down the chain from consumers to industrial and service businesses at every level of interaction. As we'll see in the next chapter, it's inevitable that all aspects of business will be affected by the change because the very baby boomers demanding them will be moving into positions of power in corporate America.

New microcomputer technologies have been developed to allow businesses to meet individualized needs at lower and lower costs. Leading-edge companies have recognized the power and potential of new software. Better design and the use of information or software increase the utility, customization, and efficiency of products. It won't be long before the entire economy is forced to pay attention to the consumer in the same way. Even if nothing else matters, it will be these leading-edge companies driving the trend because they will be taking over the important markets.

You will find, in general, that all aspects of business will see a greater concentration on software and intangible factors to add value to products and services while during this time there will be less concentration on hardware and tangible inputs. Increasingly in microcomputers, the computer itself—the hardware—is becoming more and more standardized and lower and lower in cost. In fact, most consumers only need one reasonably priced desktop or notebook computer. With that they can spend endless amounts of money buying different software packages and specialized peripheral products. The point is, software is the customizing principle, and tangible factors are minimized in quantity and cost in the equation.

You'll get to a point where you'll spend less than a hundred dollars for a computer in 20 years and spend thousands on customizing software to make money in your business or in your personal life. If you are in a hardware business and you're not adding value by better design and better information via software and other intangible factors like better marketing and service, then you are likely to experience difficulty in the boom.

We can take this software-hardware analogy to all products and services in all functions of business. Any product or service that is more intangible and serves to customize or increase the options to consumers is acting more like software. Any product or service that represents a standardized, tangible component is like the hardware. Functions in business like R&D, marketing, promotion, management, and customer service are all more software-like, or intangible. These are the areas that are going to grow in businesses. All raw material and hardware inputs, and therefore functions like production and purchasing, are going to continue to shrink.

For example, consider what the trend toward software means for business management. It means you can literally program your business for success. Franchising is a great example of this. A businessperson analyzes the key success factors for a typical mom-and-pop business and then programs that information into management software that we call a franchise agreement. Such programs for business have taken one unsophisticated mom-and-pop business after the next and achieved success rates of 90 to 97 percent. This compares to 10 to 20 percent when the business is run only on the instincts of the owner. Now that's innovation and productivity.

Companies that learn to use new technologies and management methods early will have the advantage as premium markets spread into the mainstream. And don't forget the clear history of new technologies: What appears theoretical or too costly today will almost inevitably be rendered concrete and less expensive by newer technologies as they proceed down their cost curves.

Blue-chip chips

Here's an example of a company I watched go from a conventional, standardized hardware company to a software company. This simple small-company example contains all the implications for the future of customizing.

A client of mine once manufactured camshafts for high-performance cars. If the customer, usually an owner of an early-model high-performance car, wanted to squeeze 30 to 40 extra horsepower from his engine, he paid my client $100 to $200 for a high-performance camshaft and as high as $600 for the labor-intensive process of installing the cam in the car—which meant pulling the engine.

But times have changed. Late-model car buyers cannot just

purchase a camshaft off the shelf for their car, as the computer won't recognize it and use it properly.

So my client decided to invest in a more software-intensive approach to creating horsepower. He hired some software techies to reverse-engineer the computer chips used in engines. He found he could isolate elements on that chip that made the standard camshaft perform better. He also discovered he could redesign the chip to tune the engine for high performance.

Of course, my client was delighted with the discovery. He customized computer chips for any car model. He even improved upon the manufacturer's chip design and produced 20- to 30-horsepower gains for the typical car. He sells them to very happy customers for around $120, which is a heck of a buy for 20 to 30 horsepower when you compare it with $800 for 30 to 40 horsepower. And the customer can install the chip without dismantling the car engine.

This product could eventually be produced in stores, so that it becomes a totally customized product delivered with a maximum of personalized, responsive service. How do you accomplish this? Simple.

You put all your chip designs in a central computer at your main office. Then, in the store, you install an inexpensive chip punch machine that can duplicate one chip design at a time. Then you install a modem, which allows computers to communicate over long distances using phone lines. Finally, you use a simple software program to conduct business over long distances.

Result? Speed shop owners can say yes to every customer requirement. They maintain no inventory except for a small supply of raw chips. They punch out a customized chip and deliver it on the spot.

The customer installs the chip in five minutes.

This approach eliminates the whole distribution chain. No warehouses, no trucks, no logistics, and only a fraction of the accountants, bookkeepers, paperwork, and billing. Inventory storage in warehouses is only a bad memory. The resources and workers from these indirect activities can be reallocated toward more direct customer-oriented functions in the coming decades of labor shortages.

That's the blue-chip economy in action. It means higher profits, fewer middlemen, and, most important, a direct relationship with the customer. In other words, businesspeople can take each customer's transaction and know the customer's automobile, address, demographics, and buying patterns for future marketing advantages.

It must be obvious that few people would have foreseen how something as hardware-based as performance automotive products would be a candidate for leading the way into the software age. But remember, the key impetus for change in this industry was the advent of microprocessors in auto engines. Sooner or later, a similar change in technologies will occur in your industry—if it hasn't already. The first question you should be asking is whether computers have been making invisible inroads into your products and services. We will see all products and services ultimately convert to the more software-intensive principles of the Customized Economy. So keep your eyes open.

Next you should be asking yourself this about the Customized Economy: How do I get there from here?

Strategies for survival

Based on what I've told you about the restructuring of the economy and the realignment of the world economic order, change is inevitable in the coming boom. In fact, a boom, by definition, is dramatic change. The trend for the '80s was to develop niches that would provide premium quality for a premium price. The trend for the '90s will be to develop premium-quality products at value/discount prices—bringing luxury into the affordability range of the upper middle class and ultimately the middle class by building a blue-chip economy.

Let's discuss each of the three sectors of the present economy, starting with the yellow segment. I don't want to overstate this, but . . .

Yellow companies . . .
change or die!

The vulnerable companies in the new economic order are the old, standardized yellow ones. For them, the squeeze is on right now between the blue-chip and red segments. Together those two types of businesses will form the blue-chip economy, which has no room for the yellow.

The situation is dire for these yellow businesses. The outlook is either change or die! Either alternative requires action. And soon.

The yellow company must first of all assess. Here's the question the ownership of every standardized company must ask: Is it too late in the game to become a red, value/discount company? If the answer is yes, prepare to sell your company or exit your industry— we'll discuss this in alternative No. 2. If the answer is no, proceed to . . .

Yellow alternative No. 1. *Restructure to a red company* Forget about trying to move into the blue-chip, premium-quality segment of the economy. As a rule, you can't even think of going into blue markets if you can't compete in your own markets with red companies. So you must first become red, because it's the path of least resistance and because—in my structure of business organization—it's closer to yellow than blue. If a yellow company can—and, more important, will—make the human, organizational, and technological investments, it is possible to catch up with its red competitors.

It's been done. One example comes from the world of pizza. Domino's really rattled Pizza Hut. In response, the Hut started delivering and offering drive-up service, such as it is, or can be, in pizza. Pizza Hut is now gaining back on Domino's, which has been forced into laying off people as this is being written.

> If Sears and Chrysler somehow miraculously survive as name brands in the coming boom, it will be because they restructured so dramatically they no longer are the same companies.

McDonald's has become somewhat of a yellow company since the death of Ray Kroc. Taco Bell is just getting an edge on them, but it's not too late for McDonald's to adapt to the red sector and employ the strategies outlined below. General Motors is on the cusp, but it is clearly not too late to become a mainstream survivor in the car industry. For example, I expect two things may happen during this recession to push GM out of the yellow sector and into a red strategy. First, the severity of the recession will probably give management a freer rein to take the ax more radically to GM's bureaucracy. As of May 1992, we have already seen major restructuring moves, including placing major divisions of GM on the selling block as the company consolidated during the pinch of the recession.

> Second, we are likely to see some type of merger between GM and Chrysler during the recession as Chrysler struggles to survive at its size, but has an edge in new product development that could be capitalized on by GM with its stronger financial and marketing systems. In fact, if GM underwent the same level of reorganization in this recession as Iacocca achieved for Chrysler in the recession of the early '80s, GM could be a serious world competitor in the long term.

These and the other yellow competitors have to decide whether it's too late to retool and restructure and regain enough leverage to become a red competitor. And if it is not too late, that is the only strategy, period. If you're in the yellow sector, make the move to red. Don't even think about blue.

If that move to red is too far, proceed to . . .

Yellow alternative No. 2. *Sell out while you can*   If it's too late for restructuring, then a yellow company can only bite the bullet and sell while they still can recover partial value on the dollar. When Sears management finally realizes the company can't beat Wal-Mart et al., they ought to be approaching them hat in hand. They ought to say, "Look we've got stores and other assets including a customer base. How can we joint-venture here? Don't you want to buy us out? We're not going to charge full price. Don't you want to at least buy out the auto and tire stores, the Craftsman tool line, or the Kenmore line of reliable appliances? Or don't you just want to acquire our stores, redecorate, and expand your market share?"

Like Firestone, which sold out to Bridgestone, Sears will sooner or later have to admit they're not going to make it. Firestone didn't have a chance. Even Bridgestone hasn't been able to turn them around, they're such losers. Sears will travel the same road—or change dramatically.

Taking the blue-chip company mainstream

You might suppose that the niche player, the entrepreneurial, innovative, creative company raised from a brilliant idea by a bunch of mavericks in a basement laboratory, would be the easiest to take into the blue-chip economy. Not so. Story after story is told of the tiny company that roars from anonymity to show up the big boys who wouldn't listen to the entrepreneur's ideas when he worked for them. Then what happens? Does the entrepreneur blow the big boys out of the water? Nope. The entrepreneur, often lacking the first clue about how to organize, market, and compete in the mainstream, sinks slowly—or even rapidly—into the sunset.

In my experience, you can find enormous numbers of examples of innovators incapable of managing the company once it outgrows the basement lab. You could point to Henry Ford, who innovated the assembly line and tried to run his company like a personal fiefdom. When cars finally achieved his vision of moving squarely into the mainstream, GM had become the mainstream car company in America. How? GM innovated systematic, hierarchical management and functional organization in the 1920s and became the best managed and marketed car in the world. Let's look at some of the possibilities the entrepreneurial innovators can use to exploit their blue-chip potential as the S-Curve moves toward the mainstream.

Blue-chip possibility No. 1. *Jump to a higher niche* This

strategy would apply to companies already in premium markets. This is the most dangerous and potentially the least profitable possibility when red companies begin invading your exclusive niche. By moving into a more exclusive niche, you're saying you don't want to compete head to head with a new red competitor like Lexus. Hopefully, you go into a higher, narrower niche to try to make more margins. This is exactly the strategy Porsche and BMW are trying now that Lexus has introduced a $40,000 counterpart to their $60,000 premium cars. People who want equivalent luxury for $10,000 to $20,000 less are only too happy to pay less. So BMW now intends to offer luxury in the $90,000 range with its 800 series, as does Mercedes with its new S series.

It's a nice idea, and it will probably work for a while. But BMW and you, if your choose this option, are subject to the danger that the invading company won't surrender that niche to you either. There's no question that Lexus is going to come up with a higher-end car. They're going to chase BMW, again offering equivalent luxury for $10,000 to $20,000 less. Acura already has the NSX in the $60,000 to $70,000 range competing with the $90,000 BMW 800 series and the 500 SL sports cars from Mercedes.

Blue-chip possibility No. 2. *Jump to new niches* This possibility simply means taking stock of reality and accepting it. The entrepreneurial firm, in effect, says, "We are an entrepreneurial company and we accept that. What we're good at is targeting new niches and markets. Our business is the 0 to 10 percent phase of the S-Curve. We know how to develop leading-edge products for those niches. Once that is done, our job is over. If those niches are going to move into the mainstream, we sell out or joint-venture with a larger company in the mainstream. We'll let them run a mainstream premium-quality company. We're not mainstream people."

Instead of learning an entirely new corporate culture, the entrepreneurial company might maintain a consulting partnership with an existing mainstream company. They might continue to refine research and development so the leading-edge technology never flags.

Or the entrepreneurial company might entirely sell off or license the rights to their niche products and abandon it. Then what? Of course, it can be a great strategy for the company to go on developing new 0 to 10 percent niche markets in other areas related to its customer or technical expertise. There's always a possibility that the company can again license or sell off later. Entrepreneurs could very easily make a successful career of jumping from niche to niche.

Blue-chip possibility No. 3. *Ride off into the mainstream* A third possibility for the entrepreneurial company is to commit to the mainstream conversion. Here, the decision maker says, "Our company invented this product and took command of this niche. Now that it is moving up the S-Curve into the mainstream, we are hanging on for the ride. We will fight off the red companies trying to break into our share. We intend to win this fight and dominate the marketplace or at least a clear segment of it."

When an entrepreneurial company decides to grow into a blue-chip, premium-quality company, it must become serious about management and structure. This is not optional. They must commit to refining the product continually, introducing new technologies and more efficient economies of scale to bring the cost of premium quality down.

An apparent example of success in this is Federal Express. Fred Smith built FedEx up as an entrepreneurial company, dominated his niche, and grew into the mainstream. He did it by bringing in a professional management team so his original, entrepreneurial team didn't have to learn by trial and error, always an inefficient proposition. He acquired international companies to give them international focus. He positioned Federal Express to grow into the mainstream and compete with UPS and other, larger companies. Whether that will succeed or not is not yet clear. But that's the strategy.

Blue-chip possibility No. 4. *Partner up with a red company*
No doubt you could see the danger in pursuing possibility No. 3. You must build your organization and management structure quickly and grow fast. If you don't achieve economies of scale before the competition catches on, you could find a serious red company in bed with you, uninvited. Again, look what Toyota did to BMW with its new Lexus division in the premium-quality segment of the automobile industry. Look what happened to the People's Express airline. American and United suddenly got serious about People's when they started targeting their coveted business customers. People's had an especially difficult time fighting back. The smaller company didn't have a professional and systematic management structure and did not have the large-scale strategic advantages American and United had (control of the worldwide reservations system). People's had an entrepreneurial structure. Along came a couple of giants who punched People's in the nose. They burst into flames and fell out of the skies.

Combining a blue-chip company's product-design capabilities and their focus on customers with a red company kept at arm's length might work very well. Big brother should be able to provide less expensive sales and distribution structures and lower-cost production capability. The red partner can contribute basic R&D to the smaller partner or even grant the small company access to leading-edge marketing and prospecting data bases in the industry. Such an alliance can give both companies the best of both worlds—customized products and low cost.

Blue-chip possibility No. 5. *Build a large alliance of blue-chippers* Another blue-chip strategy is to become big by piecing together a number of smaller entities. These can share a larger sales force, production facilities, management and support staff, and basic R&D facilities to build economies of scale. Companies can achieve the necessary economies of scale not only by growing a single niche to the maximum but also by bunching many related niches into an overall alliance. So you can see that it can be done either way. Small companies can build a large-scale function shared by a number of niche players. Or companies with large-scale functions can ally with a lot of smaller niche companies that can share the advantages of those functions.

A quick example. A client of mine, a small specialty publisher, was perplexed by the enormous sales costs it was paying to get its books through the complexities of the distribution chain into the bookstores. The publisher touched base with a number of other specialty publishers and found they were singing the same sad song. So they formed a new, separate distribution division. It now sells and distributes books for more than forty specialty publishers, appealing to the same segment of buyers in the book industry. All these companies share a single sales force. With their combined marketing and distribution division, they have the ability to develop a focus and to cut their sales costs by as much as 50 percent. Together they now have a broad enough line of books to interest most buyers. Yet all forty publishers maintain independent editorial control. Each still controls its own marketing and promotion programs to cater to its individual niche audiences.

An alliance of small companies can muster the clout where it counts. Yet each company can remain small and faithful to its own niche. You only want to be big where it counts and where customers don't feel the bigness. Big alienates customers by generating hierarchies and bureaucracies. Big removes the personalized touch that is to become so important in the new economy of the inner-directed baby boom generation.

Blue-Chip possibility No. 6. *Build a niche at a time* Certain niche businesses lend themselves to incremental growth into the mainstream. For example, I'm interested in music. I have found a record label, Windham Hill, that has brought together a number of leading-edge musicians who appeal to a similar audience. I know when I see its label that it is quality music because Windham Hill doesn't represent bad musicians. Once the company built a niche in acoustical music, they spun off a jazz division that also appeals to sophisticated listeners—some of which will come from their present audience and some will be attracted from new audiences.

A company can expand by moving into related niches that allow it to continue to take advantage of existing economies of scale. The more niches, the more important these economies become. If a record label ends up having hundreds of artists behind them in twenty niches they are going to be able to bring down the price of the music. They are going to be able to do mainstream advertising. They are going to have clout over the record stores. They are going to be a mainstream blue-chip company.

Many red companies will stay in the driver's seat.

Which is the best position to be in for the coming economy?

If my earlier remarks haven't already tipped you off, the answer—which is a surprise to many because my forecast overwhelmingly favors blue-chip sectors—is *red*. Remember, yellow companies will find it almost impossible to go directly to blue-chip. Niche companies almost always grow up in the entrepreneurial culture, which is great for innovating. But it takes a major shift in attitude, practice, culture, organization, and structure for a niche company to move into the mainstream. I have found that few successful entrepreneurial managers can make this transition.

So the advantage is with the red companies, which have already learned incremental techniques to improve their structure and organization to blow away their yellow competitors. How do they do this? By employing the latest technologies. By streamlining manufacturing, distribution, and management. By building in quality. By offering improved service to the overall package. All at a competitive price.

Let's look at the strategies available to red companies. As we do, keep in mind that, while many of the strategies and possibilities mentioned above are exclusive of the others, the red company should try to pursue all these strategies at the same time.

Red strategy No. 1. *Move overseas* A red company by definition is leading a maturing industry that's being captured from yellow competitors. If you're already such a leader, look at our global scenario. Identify foreign markets where your standardized goods will still grow and sell. Look first to other developed countries like Western Europe, Korea, and Japan. Then look to Mexico, Eastern Europe, the Third World countries around the Pacific Rim. In other words, follow the path of least resistance, as McDonald's has done. You don't have to innovate significantly, except to adapt to local conditions and customs. Expand what already works in the United States to countries that have not yet come up with their own S-Curve in department stores or pizzas or fast foods. To these countries, a red product is really a new and exciting blue product.

Red strategy No. 2. *Enter blue-chip markets* Red companies have to enter blue-chip markets. This is not an option if they want to survive the coming decades as leaders in their industries. The blue-chip markets are going to take over, especially in the developed countries like the United States and Europe. Ten to twenty years from now the blue-chip markets will dominate most industries. Your share in blue-chip markets is ultimately going to be more important than a share in the red, standardized markets,which will ultimately decline.

Many companies have failed to develop blue-chip products in-house because they are so far removed from such upscale customers in their mass-market red companies. When consulting to a national distiller, I saw many traditional scotch companies trying to target the emerging premium, 12-year-old scotch whiskey market, which was led by Chivas Regal. They were typically aging their same old standard-quality scotch four more years. They labeled it "Brand X Classic" and priced it $1.00 to $2.00 below Chivas. The majority of them failed. The greatest success stories came from single-malt scotch entries like Glenlivet and Glenfiddich, who, like Lexus, came up with products superior to Chivas. In this case, they priced their liquors higher than Chivas to bolster that quality position in a market where price is the positioning because few customers can distinguish a difference between quality scotches.

Red strategy No. 3. *Buy into blue-chip markets* Why should a red company reinvent the wheel? Why develop every niche from concept through R&D through prototype, test marketing, refinement, production, sales, distribution, and marketing? It's an expensive, time-consuming process—and not something red companies, in general, excel at. Toyota is more of the exception than the rule.

Management in a red company ought to be asking, "If we're the best mass-marketers with all the strategic advantages in this broad industry, why don't we joint-venture with or buy companies? Why don't we find companies that already have a proven leading-edge product and a quality image in the niche markets where we want to be? How could we then help that product grow into the main-stream? What strategic advantages do we have to offer?

If BMW could have seen the Lexus coming, they might have approached Toyota or Nissan and said, "Look, we see the hand-writing on the wall. You're the most efficient auto producers and you've got the best distribution system. We've got the best design and the best sensitivity to the quality customer. Why don't we become your design and R&D departments for luxury cars? You become the producers and distributors. Let's joint-venture."

McDonald's growth is clearly slowing in the United States. If they bought some of the specialty and gourmet fast-food outlets and gave them the wherewithal to grow and to continue to deliver consistently good food and service while turning Ronald McDonald loose on the Third World . . .

You get my point.

Macrostrategies in the global economy

In Chapter 7, we discussed the global boom scenario and the re-alignment of economic powers into three distinct centers. First and most powerful is the United States as the focal point in alliance with Canada and Mexico. Second is the European community, led by Germany, in alliance with Eastern Europe and North Africa. Third is the Far Eastern center, possibly led by Japan, with the Four Tigers and Third World countries on the Pacific Rim as economic allies.

The United States is an emerging blue-chip economy. That's where we're strongest. We dominate in the blue-chip industries because we have more markets for blue products and services and more technologies emerging from the entrepreneurial segment of the S-Curve. Our baby boomers are buying into the Customized Economy, strengthening it. Eventually, they will insist on it.

We also have several basic industries in the standardized, yellow segment that could adapt to the red, value/discount segment on the way to becoming blue-chip—if they move in time.

> The trick for the United States in the '90s is to form alliances between blue-chip and red sectors of industries to solidify global economic leadership. We are the only country that has strong world-class leaders in both sectors in a broad array of industries.

The strongest single strategy for the United States is to pair the strength of its red multinational companies with the innovativeness and market awareness of its growing blue entrepreneurial sector. That is the strategy that will assure that the United States beats both Europe and Japan. Both of those regions have strong multinational sectors, but Japan doesn't have an entrepreneurial sector to speak of, and Europe's emerging sector isn't as strong or as advanced as that in the United States. That's our ace in the hole. If we can put our indomitable entrepreneurialism together with the power of our multinational presence in the world, we'll dominate economically.

U.S. companies will have to realize that their strengths will have to be exploited in taking red companies into the blue-chip economy. Wal-Mart is the world's leading retailer, for example, and Merck is the master in pharmaceuticals and biotechnology. We still have the leading computer company, IBM, even though it's showing some initial signs of faltering. We need alliances between our red and blue companies to continue to dominate as the blue-chip sector grows stronger. And of course, IBM is being forced into alliances with companies like Apple to shore up its faltering market position. We have to realize our strength: we're holding the absolute best entrepreneurial companies in the world.

If our red companies don't enter into these alliances at home, guess who will. The Europeans and Japanese. Again, bet on it.

Japan, being primarily red, will be looking for joint ventures to get into blue markets by buying North American or European firms. It will be hard for them to develop niche companies on their own and turn them into blue-chip enterprises because their culture doesn't promote entrepreneurialism—it promotes teamwork and conformity. Yes, the Lexus is a definite entry into the premium luxury market. But it's an exception; automaking is still such a hardware-intensive industry it only allows for so much customization anyhow.

We can't afford to have the Japanese buy our best niche competitors. Europe, being mostly yellow, will probably want to joint-venture with Japanese firms to take advantage of Japan's know-how in converting yellow to red. Europeans, too often locked into their craft ethic, will have to buy into the best possible technologies for efficiently creating standardized products at value prices. Only then can they make the next move into creating a blue-chip economy. Red and yellow European firms will also be looking to joint-venture with our blue firms to get into the growing customized markets. Their blue-chip companies will also be looking for alliances with our blue-chip companies.

For companies seriously considering any of the alliances and options we've suggested here, there's probably no better time than during this worldwide recession. Recessions bring reality to all companies. Many of them are far more likely to consider such options more openly than they would when cruising ahead during good times. And, of course, many good companies' products or assets may be had at very favorable terms during such a downturn.

The trend toward strategic alliances of all types will continue as companies reorganize to meet the complex demands of the Customized Economy, baby boom workers and consumers, and the challenge of the world marketplace. But the best organizations, not the best products, will tend to win the battle for the new markets in this boom period. In Chapter 11 we'll take a summary look at the wave of organizational innovation that will distinguish this unprecedented boom period.

11

Reinventing Corporations

The Organization Wave
predicts new business
structures

BULLETIN

The old way of supervising with command and control hierarchies and ponderous bureaucracies is out. The new Customized Economy demands front-line organizations that entrepreneurs have already pioneered. The competitive edge in business will switch from the best products to the best delivery systems, which means organizational innovation will be the critical battlefield. The leaders going into the greatest boom in history will be those who don't wait for the inevitable change.

The Generation Wave revisited

I introduce a new tool in this chapter, the Organization Wave, the final component of the Generation Wave. The Organization Wave represents the shift in power that will result as members of the baby boom generation move into the leadership of corporate America.

With the Organization Wave, the picture is complete—and so elegantly simple. The first of four waves merely showed us the shape of the curve of a generation's births. The second wave described the influence of that generation's innovations on the economy. The third wave showed us the dramatic power of spending by a generation. The fourth wave represents the power of power.

Once they assume corporate leadership, baby boomers will face the new economy—and they will bring new solutions based on their entirely different history and experience as a generation growing up. Companies will be forced to shift toward new forms of organization. Long after the boom, organizational change will remain the focus of competition. The baby boom will finally get to engineer types of organizations that fit their skills, technologies, and lifestyle preferences after decades of trying to fit into the last generation's command and control hierarchies. Many have fled to

The Baby Boom Generation Wave

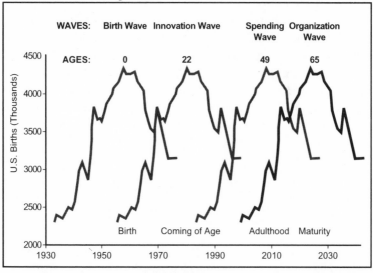

Figure 11-1. The Organization Wave of baby boomers shows us the timetable on which this generation will take power and restructure corporations

smaller, entrepreneurial businesses or have started their own businesses.

History tells us a couple of things about power. First, young people may certainly garner the visibility of change and leadership. But power is in the hands of older people. So really strong gains in productivity don't immediately follow a technological revolution. Organizations must first change to accommodate those new technologies. Of course, this change doesn't come about until the new generation takes control of the power structure. As to the second thing history tells us about power—however the shift is going to be accomplished, the baby boom generation will soon bring its own set of values to the boardrooms and corporate office suites of America. By 1995 baby boomers will comprise about 75 percent of the work force. Then we'll see the first period in which the typical manager will be a baby boomer rather than someone from the old generation. Baby boom technologies will continue to move into the mainstream economy, and that economy will continue to evolve toward customization.

When baby boomers achieve a critical mass in corporate leadership between 1995 and 2010 or so, we will see a virtual revolution in the way organizations are structured and run. It would be difficult to overstate the effect of this restructuring. It means moving away from standardization toward customization, away from hierarchy and command and control methods toward entrepreneurial structures and front-line decision making.

The look of the leading-edge entrepreneurial companies

The new wave of organizational change can be seen in emerging niche companies as they move rapidly into the mainstream markets. These companies typically stress:

- Front-line decision making and organization around customers
- The elimination or automation of indirect bureaucratic work

- Self-management and entrepreneurial structures
- Real-time information systems for communications and pinpoint controls
- Strategic focus on what they do best, subcontracting everything else to strategic partners or vendors
- Strategic alliances with companies possessing complementary skills
- A management style of coaching and supporting rather than giving orders and dictating how a job should be done

These companies are characterized by a highly challenging and stimulating work environment, personalized service and customized products, rapid learning, high innovation, and a strong culture.

The corporation of the future will restructure in one of two ways

Entrepreneurial companies will evolve. They will move away from being merely niche-oriented. As niche companies emerge into the mainstream, they will have to begin thinking big. They will get more serious about achieving economies of scale and bringing costs down to allow the new products and services to penetrate broader markets while maintaining their innovativeness and focus on the customer.

Existing companies will evolve. Large, established companies will enter the profitable growth markets as they see the success of emerging entrepreneurial companies. At first, the established companies will follow the natural tendency to simply copy product technology or organizational tactics. That won't always work. Remember when Sears declared themselves a discounter to compete with Wal-Mart? That couldn't work without fundamental change.

And what kind of organization will both these types evolve toward? I call it the corporation of the future—or the network structure—and Figure 11-2 shows what it looks like.

This figure illustrates the organizational format that will allow both centralization and decentralization at once. The left column of decentralized units labeled *a* through *h* represents company or product teams that specialize in serving corresponding distinct market segments *aa* through *hh,* offering the best of customization and personal contact. The corporation of the future achieves economies of scale by providing centralized services common to most units and market segments. Figure 11-3 elaborates on these functions.

This structure will permit companies to achieve economies of scale while not sacrificing responsiveness. The chief decentralizing functions involve many autonomous small-business units. These

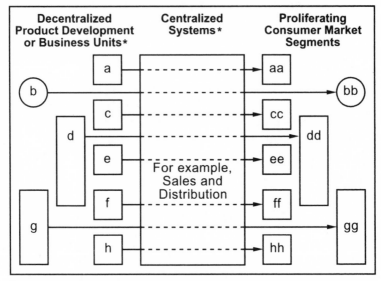

* See Figure 11-3 for a chart of these units and systems

Figure 11-2. The corporation of the future

deliver products and services that satisfy the needs of the ever-smaller segments of customers. These units share the centralized, large-scale operations necessary for cost-effectively serving such fragmented market segments where economies of scale are still critical. The key is to delegate to the small units the functions that have to do with the product and customer interface—including production whenever economy of scale factors do not prevent it.

The two possibilities I've mentioned that allow the evolution into the corporation of the future certainly aren't the only means of achieving that kind of structure. Arguably, they aren't even the best methods. For without professional help a small company with entrepreneurial roots might never learn the management skills for dealing with economies of scale that a large company already has mastered. Larger companies, on the other hand, will often fail—*have* often failed—at developing the culture and style that the entrepreneurial firm acquires by its nature.

I have had a depth of experience in both large and small companies. It is clear to me that they both have unique strengths and huge weaknesses. I came to believe that it was simply inevitable that they will learn to work together to achieve the best of both worlds rather than continuing to compete and despise each other. This will be one of the key advantages the United States can bring to the new economy—its unique combination of world-scale large corporations and its thriving entrepreneurial economy.

Small businesses can perform certain functions effectively because they can respond rapidly to changing customer needs. Functions like niche marketing, local advertising, rapid product development, and premium, personalized customer service almost always work best in smaller firms. Conversely, large companies best achieve economies of scale and mass-market standardization. Figure 11-3 summarizes some of the various functions.

Decentralized Functions	Centralized Functions
Product development	Sales and Distribution
Product R&D	Basic R&D
Marketing	Large-scale production
Advertising and PR	Information systems (MIS)
Market research	Strategic vision
Production	Strategic direction
Quality control	Funding and evaluation
Shipping	Advertising placement
Technical service	Shipping coordination
Acquisitions	Service coordination

Figure 11-3. Comparison of centralized and decentralized functions

Freeing up sales and customer service staff

The new push in technologies, especially computers, will move business toward trends like sales force automation (SFA). In SFA the sales staff on the front lines are given computer power that frees them up to serve the customer better and make more decisions. This eliminates many back-office functions. Clerical functions are programmed into the notebook computer's software so things like inventory, delivery, billing, and so on are handled completely at the contact point between sales staff and the customer.

The key focus of the corporation of the future could be summarized like this: The salesperson or "customer consultant" walks into the customer's home or office with the full capacities of the entire company in a notebook computer. The salesperson reconfigures the product or service to the customer's needs, prices it, checks credit limits, inputs orders with accuracy (with automatic checks and controls)—all the things clerical and back-office staff used to have to do. Then the customer consultant transmits the order directly over the phone lines to a flexible production facility, so that the order goes out that day or the next. Better yet, the salesperson spits out the report or service right in front of the customer, if it is an information service. Or even one step further, you provide customers with software that allows them to directly analyze their needs and place orders into your system without sales staff assistance.

Automation that eliminates bureaucracy

Just as the automation of manufacturing will be mandated by the shrinking labor force, the automation of organizations is inevitable. There simply will not be enough people available to maintain gargantuan clerical and hierarchical organizations. And your customers will not pay for the costs of such bureaucracy. But more important is that baby boomers do not work well in bureaucratic organizations. Bureaucracy is the enemy of customization! Our leading-edge small and large companies have proven that companies run more responsibly and efficiently with lower central and office staffs.

In the past two decades we have made our investments in automation where they have had the least impact on the customer. We have put computers to work to make our huge bureaucratic staffs a little more efficient—word processing, accounting, financial spreadsheets, and so on. The least investment has gone into our sales and customer service personnel, the very people who affect our customers the most. This is why our investments in computerization in the '70s and '80s produced such minor productivity gains.

> The greatest benefit of sales and field automation comes not just from making these key employees more productive and allowing them to provide better service to customers but from eliminating the huge bureaucracies and costs behind them!

The new breed of front-line managers

Until now, the primary function of managers has been supervision—telling employees what to do and measuring how well they do it. But the new breed of individualistic employees increasingly don't want to be or need to be supervised. It's not that employees always make the right decisions. But as we have learned through the resounding success of free-market economies, the greatest motivation and the greatest number of good decisions come when people are free to exercise judgment in their own sphere of authority.

Where companies have dared to foster self-management, the hard numbers have shown dramatic improvements in productivity—up to 40 and 50 percent. The key principle is that the people closest to customers are most sensitive to their needs. They make better decisions than remote executives when they have the necessary skills and information. This means that executives must:

Focus on organizing cross-functional teams with the range of skills needed to solve customer or operational problems
Provide training, resources, information, and performance feedback
Delegate most decision-making authority
Hold teams accountable for results

Look for managers and professional staff members to be reduced in numbers at the top and increasingly put into front-line teams where they are more action-oriented and accountable to customers. Look for upper-level roles to change as well. The better top managers will not make decisions for employees and departments under them. Instead they will teach their employees how to think like managers and, hence, make their own decisions. This means that no matter how much we delegate, we will still need many people with managerial and professional skills. They'll spend more time teaching and coaching and will make fewer decisions for their subordinate employees.

> The truth is that we will need *more* managerial and professional people. But these *must* come equipped with human skills, not just technical. Top-level management will have their hands full with their new roles in overseeing complex networks of relationships and alliances and designing information and training systems to glue them together. Many more managers and professionals will move their skills closer to the front lines, where the real action will be, performing within small cross-functional teams that make decisions closer to the customer.

The secret to customization

The secret to customization is no secret at all: Organize your entire company around your front-line sales and service personnel who serve customers. Your goal must be to provide the best desired service at costs and prices that are affordable—that is what competing in the Customized Economy is all about! And you can't simply make huge investments in your sales force and accomplish this. You can get higher levels of service, but you often can only do it at high costs—unless you design your systems to eliminate bureaucratic inputs and functions and the huge costs and delays that often go with them.

All successful management must ask: What can be done so our company will make every decision at the lowest level possible and add as much value as possible to our product or service on the front lines with as little impact and interference from back-line departments?

CEOs must give their companies clear strategy and direction. Beyond that they should not make operational decisions. CEOs should dedicate themselves to giving employees the information, the tools, and the training to make decisions in direct response to customers.

CEOs in the corporation of the future should question every decision or information process that is not conducted on the front lines of their companies. Their vision for their companies should be: How can I train my front-line employees and provide them with the vision and information necessary to make the same decisions I would make if I were on the front line serving the customers. This means surrendering the old command and control style and taking on the discipline of letting front-line people make decisions and make mistakes which will allow them to learn.

Only when you can provide real customization and responsive, human service near the front will you have mastered the secret to doing it ultimately at the lowest costs. This means the automation or elimination of most clerical and back-office jobs, where the majority of employees work! But it doesn't mean high unemployment, except during this recession. We will be growing dramatically in the rest of the '90s and beyond. So we will urgently need this clerical automation to free us to expand the number of jobs that serve the customized needs of the customer more directly. Most clerical people should be encouraged to shift into more direct functions like sales, customer service, design, marketing, and production—things that the customer feels directly and is willing to pay for. This is not bad, for it means more interesting and fulfilling jobs!

The typical clerical worker now enters information into a computer or does bookkeeping. In the corporation of the future they will use their systematic skills and knowledge of the company and its products to answer phone inquiries from customers. They will handle phone or field orders that require order entry and customized pricing or configuration. This ultimately means that clerical workers must fortify their clerical skills with more human ones—learning to interact with and serve the customer—whether it be the final customer or a department within the company that is their customer.

The need for human skills

Why are the technical skills not going to be so important? Our software systems and engineering systems will be increasingly such that computers will calculate figures, do the paperwork, and handle all the technical manipulations. All most employees will have to do is be minimally functional on a computer and be able to do simple, user-friendly programs. Even the lack of typing skills won't be a setback in the future. We already have computers that use touch screens. A newer generation will recognize handwriting commands from an electronic pen. And voice-activated programs are already affordable in the retail marketplace. These computer innovations will handle the left-brain functions, those of calculating figures and storing volumes of data. Most things that can be done by the left brain alone, as a general rule, will be fully automated in the next twenty years.

The key job will be to solve customer problems creatively using right-brain functions. Can you use your intuitive powers? Can you solve complex personal problems? Are you sensitive to the needs of customers? Can you provide personalized service? Can you identify new customer needs and develop and test new products to meet them? Those call for the right brain or creative faculties, which will be valued in the corporation of the future.

This brings up another important concern. Some analysts are telling us that if we don't become a computer programmer or some high-tech junkie, we won't have a job in the future. Because the Japanese have so many math junkies they're the ones who will have the jobs. I'll concede that it's certainly true we're going to need more computer programmers, more technical people, and more engineers. But what I see in this time of customer orientation and the customized corporation is a vast need for the more important skill of dealing with people. People who have such human skills as solving human problems instead of math equations and those who like dealing with employees and customers instead of numbers will be in high demand.

The number one management concern

Human resource management and motivation is fundamentally a matter of taking the time to find out what truly motivates each employee. What are his or her "core desires"? In other words, managers should design jobs and structures around the individual needs and motivation of employees rather than fitting everyone into standardized job descriptions and systems. A manager should have two major goals: first to hire people who fit the company's corporate culture and second to make sure that each employee is ultimately placed in the job that best fits his or her unique desires and skills.

The future of corporations

What we will be seeing in the future is the emergence of the corporate society—where large and small corporate networks become the basic social and community unit. Such diverse structures will combine large and small business and a full range of job opportunities. They will often be dispersed with central management and professional units in the big cities. But many sales and customer service units will be spread throughout the world. And many front-line-oriented staff consulting units will be located out in small towns and cities where the worker prefers to live. All of these segments will be connected by a common information system that keeps everyone in touch with everyone else. It will continually update everyone on what everyone else is doing—in real time. Obviously that means communication is instantaneous and synchronous. More important, it helps solidify a common overall mission and culture with dispersed units having the freedom to develop in the localized cultures they need for their customers. Many more people will work in their homes part-time or full-time. Many other departments will be located in neighborhoods where people can be close to each other for work and social reasons with a minimum of commuting time and costs.

Look forward, think forward

The key to work changes will be moving toward these goals as quoted by Stan Davis in *2020 Vision:* "Every Customer a Market" and "Every Employee a Business." We are going to see the Megatrends first cited by John Naisbitt in the '80s *accelerate* and move into work and the marketplace far faster than they did in the past two decades. Look for customized products made and serviced by highly focused, highly self-managed networks of diverse companies, suppliers, and management systems groups.

You have to find your place in this system. Are you an entrepreneur, a customer-oriented sales or service type, a strategic planner, an information provider, or a systems designer? These are the types of creative functions the new economy is going to need—not order takers, not paper pushers, not back-office analysts. If your job function is primarily bureaucratic, you may be an endangered species like the northern spotted owl. The United States has the best mix of the new creative skills and the leading markets for such customized and specialty products. Therefore we should lead world markets again, although nothing like in the 1950s, when we had no competition as Europe and Japan were devastated by World War II.

Do I expect the remarkable changes in organization to occur overnight? No. Of course not. The change in the ways we organize can only occur gradually as the Individualist generation assumes power from the generation of Bob Hope. And such human and cultural changes necessarily take time and persistence to accomplish.

The leading-edge companies, those spawned in the entrepreneurial revolution of the '70s and '80s, have already proven that it can be done. Companies like Cypress Semiconductor have already moved into the Customized Economy. You can also see companies like General Electric and Johnson & Johnson under the leadership of progressive CEOs like Jack Welch and Ralph Larsen, pushing the envelope for larger organizations. And I have even seen small, regional companies in very basic industries doing it—like Granite Rock Company in Watsonville, California, and Krueger International office furniture in Green Bay, Wisconsin. Any company can make radical strides in this direction.

Yes, human change is difficult to initiate. And changes in management and hands-off leadership are difficult to accomplish, so most companies wait or choose to change gradually. The '90s won't wait for laggards, though. Companies that dally may pay a high price in the loss of a competitive edge. They simply may not be around to talk about it.

Organizations with the visionary leadership of T. J. Rodgers at Cypress Semiconductor will adapt to the Customized Economy by developing new skills in managers and employees. These skills will be directed at moving companies toward front-line management and decision-making.

Sooner or later, the shift in organizational power and the shift toward a Customized Economy will come to your industry and your business. Every company will have to make the adjustment or follow the path of the other dinosaurs of the Standardized Economy—you know, the dreaded but decaying yellow competitors. The smart choice is to be the one who gains the advantage early on in this huge competitive boom we are approaching. The very fact that human and organizational change is difficult allows you to create a sustainable competitive edge if you can apply these front-line principles to your organization early. So it's to your advantage to change sooner. And remember, there is no better time to make such changes than during the recession in 1993 and 1994.

If the change comes later, it will be when the Individualist generation of baby boomers moves into the corporate suites of America. A company does not have to risk dying or wait for the grizzled power structure of the Bob Hope generation to pass into retirement. The skills for tomorrow's brand of management can be learned. The critical management and organizational challenge will be to change from hierarchical to front-line and entrepreneurial structures. This will become the battleground and decisive strategic edge for companies to compete in the coming boom.

It is such a rich field of study in itself that it really must be the subject for another book.